DEDICATION

Miss Daisy's Tearoom dedicates this cookbook to our guests and friends who have supported the Tearoom, inspired our aims, challenged our energies, and, lastly, requested this book. We hope our efforts say it has been fun for us and perhaps inspire you to repeat a favorite meal at home.

INTRODUCTION

Our first attempt to bring you a cookbook has been completed. We have talked cookbook from dawn to dusk with the hope that our sharing with you will enrich your culinary efforts. It is interesting to note that Marilyn Lehew and Daisy King, as business partners, have presented every recipe that has ever been used in the Tearoom for use in this book. Each recipe serves six to eight people unless stated otherwise.

A tearoom operates because of a devoted staff, tempting recipes, new ideas and hard work. Miss Daisy's has been blessed with a combination of all of these. To each member of the staff, as well as friends and relatives, the Tearoom wants to say "Thanks" for making Miss Daisy's a success.

Editor and friend,

Judy Wheeler

Recipes

from

Miss Daisy's

Rutledge Hill Press
Nashville, Tennessee

ISBN: 0-934395-15-2

First published in 1978 by Miss Daisy's Tearoom. Carter's Court, Franklin, Tennessee.

Published in 1985 in Nashville, Tennessee, by Rutledge Hill Press, Inc., 211 Seventh Avenue North, Nashville, Tennessee 37219.

Second Rutledge Hill Press printing, October, 1986

Third Rutledge Hill Press printing, October, 1989

Fourth Rutledge Hill Press printing, January, 1992

Fifth Rutledge Hill Press printing, October, 1994

Sixth Rutledge Hill Press printing, September, 1997

TABLE OF CONTENTS

4

DAISY'S UPTOWN

The story of Daisy King's career in the restaurant business is as interesting as the food she serves. In the mid-1970's when Carter's Court in Franklin was still on the drawing board, the developers recognized the need for a place where ladies could come for lunch. After a turn-of-the-century house was moved back from Columbia Avenue to its present location, upon seeing it people exclaimed, "That's it. That's got to be a tearoom." Thus, the old house was given a new lease on life and with much work and ingenuity became Miss Daisy's Tearoom.

Persistence, determination, and pride were all words used to describe the opening of Miss Daisy's Tearoom. It was decided from the beginning that "only the best" quality foods would be served. No mass produced, radar range shortcuts would be taken. The menu would change several times a year, coordinating the food with the seasons. Daisy King personally greeted each customer, giving them the feeling of being both welcome and honored. It was said that although you came to Miss Daisy's as a customer, you left as a friend.

The restaurant moved to Green Hills, a suburb of Nashville, in 1982, expanding to a full-service restaurant. Daisy returned to her original Carter's Court location in 1986, with Daisy's of Carter's Court, which she later sold to new owners.

In 1989, Daisy closed the Green Hills location and moved to Daisy's Uptown in the newly developed Church Street Centre. Open daily from Monday through Saturday for lunch and dinner, as well as for appetizers and cocktails in the afternoon, Daisy's Uptown has quickly gained a reputation for its well-appointed dining room and creative menu that surprises as well as delights.

National food and restaurant writers have paid tribute to Daisy's, but more importantly, so have the citizens of Middle Tennessee. The original commitment to excellence has become a Nashville tradition.

```
┌─────────────────────────────────────────────────────┐
│                                                     │
│                  TURKEY DIVAN                       │
│                                                     │
│     FROZEN CHERRY SALAD - BRAN MUFFINS              │
│                                                     │
│              BUTTERMILK PIE                         │
│                                                     │
└─────────────────────────────────────────────────────┘
```

TURKEY DIVAN

2 10 oz. pkg. frozen broccoli or 2 bunches fresh
   broccoli (do not overcook)
2 - 3 cups cooked turkey, diced or sliced

Sauce

2 cans cream of chicken   1/2 cup shredded sharp
   soup   cheese
1 cup mayonnaise   1/2 cup toasted bread
1 tsp. lemon juice   crumbs
1/2 tsp. curry powder   1 tbsp. margarine

In a flat Pyrex dish, put a layer of broccoli and
turkey. Prepare sauce by mixing remaining ingredients. Pour sauce over broccoli and turkey.   Top
with bread crumbs and margarine.   Bake at 350 degrees for 25-30 minutes.   This can be made ahead
of time and heated.

FROZEN CHERRY SALAD

1 16 oz. can cherry pie   1 14 oz. can condensed
   filling   milk
1 14 oz. can crushed   1 13 oz. carton whipped
   pineapple   topping

Mix all ingredients.   Freeze in 9 x 13 pan.   Cut in
squares and garnish with Party Salad Topping (page 58)
and strawberry.

7

BRAN MUFFINS

2 cups boiling water
2 cups bran cereal
1 heaping cup vegetable
  shortening
3 cups sugar
4 eggs
1 quart buttermilk

5 cups flour
5 tsp. baking soda
1 tbsp. salt
4 cups bran cereal
1 15 oz. box raisins,
  optional

Add 2 cups bran cereal to the boiling water. Set
aside. Cream shortening and sugar in large bowl
of mixer. Add eggs. Beat well. Add buttermilk and
scalded bran cereal. Sift flour, baking soda and salt
salt. Add dry ingredients to liquid mixture. You
will have to transfer to a larger bowl when adding
dry ingredients. Stir in remaining bran cereal and
raisins. Bake in greased muffin tins for 15-20
minutes in a 400 degree oven. This batter keeps in
refrigerator for a month, so only bake the number
needed and refrigerate remaining batter for future
bakings.

BUTTERMILK PIE

1/3 cup butter
1 cup sugar
3 beaten egg yolks
3 tbsp. flour
1/4 tsp. salt
1 tsp. lemon juice

1/2 tsp. grated lemon
  rind
1½ cups buttermilk
3 egg whites, stiffly
  beaten
1 unbaked 9 inch pie crust

Cream butter and sugar. Add egg yolks and beat well.
Add flour, salt, lemon juice and rind. Mix thoroughly.
Add buttermilk. Fold in beaten egg whites. Pour
filling into crust and bake for 10 minutes in a 450
degree oven. Reduce heat and continue to bake 40
minutes in a 350 degree oven.

```
┌─────────────────────────────────────────────────────┐
│                    SHRIMP CREOLE                    │
│                                                     │
│   CONGEALED CUCUMBER SALAD - SALLY LUNN MUFFINS     │
│                                                     │
│                  HEATH BAR CAKE                     │
│                                                     │
└─────────────────────────────────────────────────────┘
```

SHRIMP CREOLE

1/4 cup vegetable oil	1 tbsp. sugar
1 cup diced onion	1 tbsp. salt
1 cup diced celery	1 tbsp. chili powder
1/2 cup diced green	1/8 tsp. hot sauce
pepper	2 lbs. cleaned, raw
3½ cups canned tomatoes	shrimp
1 8 oz. can tomato	1/4 cup flour
sauce	1/4 cup water
2 bay leaves	

Saute onion, celery and pepper in oil until tender.
Add tomatoes, tomato sauce, bay leaves, sugar, salt
and chili powder. Mix well. Simmer 30 minutes. Remove bay leaves. Add shrimp. Simmer an additional
30 minutes. Mix flour and water to a paste; add a
cup or two of tomato mixture and stir with wire
whisk until blended. Add flour mixture to tomato
mixture. Cook until creole is thickened - about 5
minutes. Serve over rice.

CONGEALED CUCUMBER SALAD

1 pkg. lemon gelatin	1 carton sour cream
1/2 cup hot water	1/2 cucumber, minced fine
3/4 tsp. salt	1 tbsp. lemon juice
2 tbsp. fresh lemon	
juice	

Congealed Cucumber Salad (continued)

Dissolve gelatin in hot water and really cool. Beat in sour cream with beater. Add other ingredients. Pour into mold and let congeal.

SALLY LUNN MUFFINS

1/2 cup butter
1/2 cup sugar
3 cups flour
4 tsp. baking powder
1 1/2 tsp. salt

2 cups milk
1/2 cup light cream
1/2 cup heavy cream
3 eggs, beaten

Cream butter and sugar until light. Sift dry ingredients together. Add to butter-sugar mixture, alternating with milk and cream. Add eggs. Mix well. Bake in greased muffin tins for 30 minutes in a 350 degree oven.

HEATH BAR CAKE

1 cup brown sugar
1/2 cup white sugar
1/2 cup butter
2 cups flour

1 egg
1 cup buttermilk
1 tsp. baking soda
7 Heath bars

Mix first 4 ingredients like a pie crust. Take out 1/2 cup and save. Add the egg, buttermilk and baking soda to rest of mixture. Put in a greased and floured 9 x 13 pan. Sprinkle the remaining sugar-flour-butter mixture combined with broken Heath bars over top of batter. Bake for 30 minutes in a 350 degree oven.

```
┌─────────────────────────────────────────────────┐
│                                                 │
│        CARTER'S COURT SALAD BOWL                │
│                                                 │
│        HONEY - FRENCH DRESSING                  │
│                                                 │
│  ICE CREAM PECAN BALL WITH BUTTERSCOTCH SAUCE   │
│                                                 │
└─────────────────────────────────────────────────┘
```

CARTER'S COURT SALAD BOWL

1 16 oz. carton cottage cheese
8 cups mixed salad greens
2 tomatoes, cut in wedges

4 eggs, sieved
1 cup French style green beans

Black and green olives
Asparagus spears

To arrange individual salads: put a small dip of cottage cheese in center of clear glass plate or shallow bowl about 9 inches in diameter. Put the mixed greens around the cottage cheese. Garnish with remaining ingredients. Put small amount of paprika on cottage cheese.

HONEY - FRENCH DRESSING

1 cup vegetable oil
1/4 cup vinegar
1/4 cup lemon juice
1 tsp. salt

1/2 tsp. dry mustard
1/2 tsp. paprika
1/3 cup honey

Beat all ingredients together. Keep in refrigerator. Shake well before serving.

11

ICE CREAM PECAN BALL WITH BUTTERSCOTCH SAUCE

Make 8 large ice cream balls. Roll in chopped pecans. Freeze.

Butterscotch Sauce

1½ cups light brown sugar	2/3 cup white corn syrup
4 tbsp. butter	2/3 cup evaporated milk

Combine sugar, butter and syrup. Stir constantly over low heat until sugar dissolves and mixture boils. Stop stirring. Cook until the mixture forms a soft ball in cold water (240 degrees). Cool slightly. Add evaporated milk. Pour over vanilla ice cream ball covered with chopped pecans.

```
CREAMED CHICKEN ON CORNMEAL MUFFIN RING

FESTIVE CRANBERRY SALAD - MARINATED CARROTS

FUDGE PIE WITH PEPPERMINT ICE CREAM
```

CREAMED CHICKEN

1/2 cup butter	2 cups chicken stock
1/2 cup flour	2 cups light cream
1 tsp. salt	2 cups milk

Melt butter. Add flour and salt; cook until bubbly. Add chicken stock. Stir with a wire whisk until smooth. Add cream and milk. Simmer 30 minutes. Add the following ingredients and heat thoroughly when ready to serve;

4 cups chicken, cooked and chopped	1 2 oz. jar pimento, drained and chopped
1 8 oz. can water chestnuts, sliced and drained	1/4 cup sherry

CORNMEAL MUFFIN RINGS

1 cup self-rising cornmeal	1 egg, slightly beaten
1 tbsp. flour (optional)	3 tbsp. bacon drippings or melted shortening
1 cup buttermilk	1 tsp. sugar

Mix dry ingredients. Mix buttermilk and egg and add to dry ingredients. Pour in bacon drippings or melted shortening and mix well. Bake in hot greased rings or pan about 20 minutes in a 450 degree oven.

FESTIVE CRANBERRY SALAD

1 3 oz. pkg. orange
  gelatin
1 3 oz. pkg. raspberry
  gelatin

1 16 oz. can whole berry
  cranberry sauce
1 14 oz. can crushed
  pineapple

Dissolve gelatin in 2 cups boiling water. Add the
cranberry sauce and crushed pineapple with juice.
Mix well. Put in individual molds or 9 x 9 dish.
Congeal.

MARINATED CARROTS

2 lbs. carrots
2 medium onions, diced
2 green peppers, chopped
1 can tomato soup
3/4 cup vinegar

1/2 cup corn oil
1 tsp. Worcestershire
  sauce
1 tsp. prepared mustard
3/4 sugar

Prepare carrots for cooking. Slice and cook in salted
water until tender. Drain. Arrange carrots, onions
and peppers in layers. Make a marinade by combining
remaining ingredients. Pour marinade over carrots.
Refrigerate for 24 hours before serving. The marinated
carrots will keep in the refrigerator for over a week.

FUDGE PIE

2 squares unsweetened
  chocolate
1/2 cup butter
2 eggs

1 cup sugar
2 tbsp. flour
1 tsp. vanilla
1/2 cup chopped walnuts

Melt chocolate and butter. Add eggs, sugar, flour,
vanilla and nuts. Bake in greased pie pan for 30
minutes at 325 degrees, starting in cold oven.
Delicious served with peppermint ice cream!

```
┌─────────────────────────────────────────────────┐
│                                                 │
│   SHRIMP ASPIC MOLD WITH HORSERADISH DRESSING   │
│                                                 │
│          TOASTED CHEESE MUFFIN                  │
│                                                 │
│            POPPY SEED CAKE                      │
│                                                 │
└─────────────────────────────────────────────────┘
```

SHRIMP ASPIC MOLD

1 6 oz. pkg. lemon gelatin	1/2 cup chopped green olives
1½ cups boiling water	1 tbsp. minced onion
1/2 cup chili sauce	1 cup chopped celery
2 cups tomato juice	2 lbs. cooked shrimp
1 tbsp. sweet pickle relish	

Dissolve gelatin in boiling water. Add chili sauce, tomato juice. Chill until it begins to thicken. Add remaining ingredients. Congeal.

HORSERADISH DRESSING

1 cup mayonnaise	1 tbsp. horseradish
2 tbsp. chili sauce	

Mix all ingredients together. Refrigerate.

TOASTED CHEESE MUFFINS

8 oz. Cheddar cheese,
  grated
1/2 cup butter, softened
2 eggs, beaten
1/2 cup black olives,
  chopped

1 tsp. garlic salt
1 tsp. onion salt
8 English muffins, cut
  in halves

Blend all ingredients in mixer except for the English muffins. Spread mixture on cut side of muffin halves. Sprinkle with paprika. Bake 10 minutes in a 400 degree oven.

POPPY SEED CAKE

1 yellow cake mix
1 pkg. instant coconut
  pudding
1/2 cup vegetable oil
1 cup water

4 eggs
1/2 cup poppy seeds
2 cups prepared vanilla
  pudding

Mix all ingredients together with electric mixer. Bake in a greased tube pan for 1 hour in a 350 degree oven. When cool, split into three layers. Mix one package vanilla pie filling according to directions or make your own filling. Spread between layers and on top of cake. Refrigerate cake until serving time.

16

GARDEN TOMATO STUFFED WITH TEA ROOM TUNA SALAD

HOT FRENCH CHEESE SANDWICHES

PECAN PIE

GARDEN TOMATO STUFFED WITH TEA ROOM TUNA SALAD

3 7 oz. cans white   1/4 cup sweet pickle
  tuna, drained   relish
1/2 cup chopped celery   1/2 cup mayonnaise
4 hard boiled eggs,   8 medium sized tomatoes
  chopped

Flake tuna. Add remaining ingredients and mix well.
Chill. The white or Albacore tuna is a must for
this salad. Prepare tomatoes for stuffing. Stuff
generously with tuna.

HOT FRENCH CHEESE SANDWICHES

1/2 lb. sharp cheddar   1 tsp. garlic salt
  cheese   1 tsp. onion salt
1/2 cup butter, softened   16 slices white bread
2 eggs

In a mixer blend cheese which has been grated and
butter. Add eggs and salt. Whip until creamy.
Spread mixture on slice of bread, place another
slice of bread on top and spread it with cheese
mixture. Sprinkle with paprika. Cut into halves.
Bake 10-15 minutes in a 400 degree oven. These
may be frozen and then baked as needed.

PECAN PIE

1/2 cup sugar
2 tbsp. butter
3 eggs, beaten
1/4 tsp. salt
1 tsp. vanilla

1 cup light corn syrup
1 tbsp. flour
1 cup pecans
1 unbaked 9 inch pie
   crust

Cream sugar and butter. Add remaining ingredients. Pour into pie crust. Bake for 40 minutes in a 350 degree oven.

NOTES

REMEMBER – Each recipe serves 6 – 8, unless otherwise stated.

```
TEA ROOM CHILI

GREEN SALAD - FRENCH BREAD

SOUR CREAM POUND CAKE
```

TEA ROOM CHILI

1 lb. ground beef
1 medium onion, chopped
1/2 green pepper, diced
1 pkg. chili seasoning
   mix

1 16 oz. can tomato
   sauce with bits
1 16 oz. can chili or
   kidney beans
Water, if needed

Saute beef, onion and pepper. Add remaining
ingredients. Simmer for 2 hours before serving.

SOUR CREAM POUND CAKE

1 cup soft butter
2 cups sugar
6 eggs
3 cups sifted flour

1/2 tsp. salt
1/4 tsp. soda
1 cup sour cream
1 tsp. vanilla

Cream butter and sugar until light. Add eggs one at
a time, beating thoroughly after each. Sift dry ingredients 3 times and add alternately with sour
cream to first mixture, beating until smooth. Add
flavoring. Pour into 9 inch tube pan which has been
greased. Bake at 350 degrees for 1 hour and 20 minutes. Let stand in pan on rack about 5 minutes.
This cake freezes well.

```
┌─────────────────────────────────────────────────┐
│                                                 │
│            CORN AND HAM CHOWDER                  │
│                                                 │
│               GREEN SALAD                        │
│                                                 │
│             HOT FRUIT CRISP                      │
│                                                 │
│                                                 │
└─────────────────────────────────────────────────┘
```

CORN AND HAM CHOWDER

1/2 cup butter	1½ tsp. salt
1 cup chopped celery	1/2 tsp. pepper
1/2 cup chopped onion	1/2 tsp. onion salt
2 cups diced cooked ham	1/2 tsp. celery salt
3 10 oz. pkg. frozen	1 cup milk
cream style corn	

Saute celery, onion and ham in butter. Add remaining ingredients. Heat. Simmer 20 minutes before serving. Garnish with fresh parsley.

HOT FRUIT CRISP

1/2 cup butter, softened	1/2 tsp. cinnamon
1 cup oatmeal	1/2 tsp. nutmeg
1 cup flour	1 can apple or peach
1 cup light brown sugar	pie filling

Put pie filling in a greased 9 x 9 baking dish. Slice butter on top. Mix together oatmeal, flour, brown sugar, cinnamon and nutmeg. Sprinkle this mixture over pie filling and butter. Bake for 30 to 40 minutes in a 350 degree oven.

```
+--------------------------------------------------+
|                                                  |
|              MEXICAN CASSEROLE                   |
|                                                  |
|         GREEN SALAD - FRENCH BREAD               |
|                                                  |
|            FLOWER POT DESSERT                     |
|                                                  |
+--------------------------------------------------+
```

MEXICAN CASSEROLE

1 lb. ground beef	1 16 oz. can chili beans
1 medium onion, chopped	or kidney beans, drained
1 tbsp. salt	1 pkg. chili seasoning mix
1 tbsp. pepper	1/2 lb. sharp cheese,
1 16 oz. can tomatoes	grated
with juice	Corn chips
1 8 oz. can tomato sauce	

Saute ground beef and onion, add salt and pepper.
Add remaining ingredients except for beans, cheese
and corn chips. Cook on medium heat for 30 minutes.
Add beans. Pour into casserole and top with cheese
and corn chips. Bake 20 minutes in a 350 degree oven.

FLOWER POT DESSERT

8 sterile clay flower	Whipped topping or
pots, 2½ - 4 inch size	whipped cream
1 purchased small pound	Shaved chocolate
or angel food cake	8 5-inch straw pieces
1/2 cup dark rum or	8 fresh flowers with
2 oz. rum flavoring	some stem
1 quart cherry vanilla	
ice cream	

Flower Pot Dessert (Continued)

Sprinkle half of the rum over crumbled cake. Fill
flower pots with 1 inch of cake mixture. Mix remaining half of rum with ice cream. Put ice cream
in clay pot. Cover with whipped topping. Sprinkle
with shaved chocolate. Put straw in center of each
pot so that 3 inches are showing. Put in freezer
until serving time. Put fresh flower stem in straw
and serve.

```
┌─────────────────────────────────────────────────────┐
│                                                     │
│   FRESH FRUIT BOWL WITH POPPYSEED DRESSING          │
│                                                     │
│           FINGER SANDWICHES                         │
│                                                     │
│           LEMON SUPREME CAKE                        │
│                                                     │
└─────────────────────────────────────────────────────┘
```

FRESH FRUIT BOWL

Use any combination of the following fruits:

Peaches	Honeydew melon
Cherries	Cantaloupe
Grapes	Strawberries
Watermelon	Pineapple
Blueberries	Bananas
Grapefruit	

POPPYSEED DRESSING

3/4 cup sugar	1 cup vegetable oil
1 tsp. salt	1½ tbsp. onion juice
1 tsp. dry mustard	2 tbsp. poppy seeds

Mix dry ingredients together. Add vinegar. Mix well. Add oil and beat until thick. Add onion juice and poppy seeds. Refrigerate until ready to use.

PUMPKIN BREAD FOR FINGER SANDWICHES

1 cup water	3½ cups self-rising
1 cup oil	flour
1 can pumpkin pie filling	1 tsp. each; nutmeg,
or can plain pumpkin	ginger, salt
3 cups sugar	1/2 tsp. cloves
3 eggs	1/2 tsp. baking powder
1 cups black walnuts,	2 tsp. cinnamon
chopped	2 tsp. baking soda
1½ cups dates, chopped	

Mix first seven ingredients in large mixing bowl.
Sift together remaining ingredients. Mix well with
pumpkin mixture. Pour into two large greased loaf
pans. Bake for 1½ hours in a 325 degree oven.

LEMON SUPREME CAKE

1 box lemon supreme	1/2 cup salad oil
cake mix	1 3 oz. pkg. lemon gel-
4 eggs	atin dissolved in 1
	cup water

Mix and bake in square pan, 2 quart casserole or
tube pan at 350 degrees for 45 minutes. Top with 1
can frozen lemonade concentrate mixed with 1 cup
powdered sugar.

MISS DAISY'S BEEF CASSEROLE

GREEN SALAD - HOT FRENCH BREAD

FRESH CARROT CAKE WITH CREAM CHEESE FROSTING

MISS DAISY'S BEEF CASSEROLE

2 lbs. lean ground beef
1 cup diced celery
1/4 cup diced green
pepper
3/4 cup chopped onion
1 29 oz. can tomatoes
1 16 oz. can tomatoes
1 8 oz. can mushrooms
pieces, drained
1 8 oz. can water
chestnuts, drained
and sliced

1 cup cubed American
processed cheese
1/2 cup green olives,
chopped
1/2 cup black olives,
chopped
1/2 tsp. salt
1/4 tsp. pepper
1 6 oz. pkg. egg noodles,
uncooked
2 cups shredded Cheddar
cheese

Brown beef. Pour off any accumulated grease. Add celery, green pepper, onion and saute. Add tomatoes and their juice. Add remaining ingredients except for the Cheddar cheese. Simmer 20 minutes. Pour into 9 x 13 casserole. Spread Cheddar cheese on top. Bake for 30 minutes in a 350 degree oven.

25

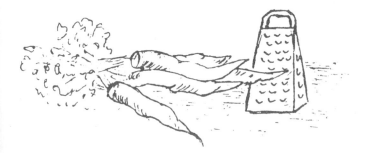

FRESH CARROT CAKE WITH CREAM CHEESE FROSTING

4 eggs
1½ cups vegetable oil
2 cups flour
2 cups sugar
2 tsp. baking powder
2 tsp. baking soda

3 tsp. cinnamon
1 tsp. salt
3 packed cups grated
   raw carrots
1/2 cup black walnuts,
   chopped

Beat eggs and oil. Mix dry ingredients. Add to egg and oil mixture. Beat well. Add carrots and walnuts. Blend. Pour into 3 greased 9 inch layer pans. Bake for 25 minutes in a 350 degree oven.

Frosting

1 lb. box confectioners'
   sugar
1 stick butter, softened

1 8 oz. pkg. cream
   cheese
1/2 cup black walnuts,
   chopped, optional

Blend ingredients. Spread on cake. Refrigerate cake.

FESTIVE SHRIMP SALAD ON TOMATO ASPIC

CRUNCHY CHEESE BISCUITS

TANGY CITRUS CAKE

FESTIVE SHRIMP SALAD

1 lb. cooked shrimp	2 tbsp. chopped pimento
1 cup chopped celery	1 tbsp. chopped green
2 fresh tomatoes, peeled	onion
and diced	1/2 tsp. salt
1/4 cup chopped green	1/8 tsp. pepper
pepper	Avocado wedges

Combine all ingredients above except avocado wedges. Mix with the sour cream dressing below. Serve on tomato aspic squares and garnish with avocado wedges.

SOUR CREAM DRESSING

1 cup sour cream	1 tbsp. lemon juice
1/2 cup catsup	2 tsp. horseradish
1 tbsp. soy sauce	1 tsp. salt
1 tbsp. grated onion	1/2 tsp. dry mustard

Blend all. Add to shrimp mixture.

TOMATO ASPIC

2 cups tomato juice	2 3 oz. pkgs. lemon
1/2 cups chili sauce	gelatin
1½ cups boiling water	

Dissolve gelatin in boiling water. Add other ingredients. Pour in 9 x 9 pan. Congeal.

CRUNCHY CHEESE BISCUITS

1/2 cup butter	1/2 tsp. salt
1 cup grated sharp	1 cup plain flour
cheddar cheese	1 cup crispy rice cereal

Blend butter and flour. Add cheese and salt. Mix well. Add rice cereal. Make into balls and bake for about 10 minutes in a 350 degree oven.

TANGY CITRUS CAKE

| 2 medium oranges | 2 eggs |
| 1 lemon cake mix | Sweetened whipped cream |

Grate, peel and squeeze juice from oranges. Add enough water to orange juice to measure 1 1/3 cups. Blend cake mix (dry), eggs, orange peel and juice mixture in bowl on low speed about 1/2 minute. Beat on medium speed 3 minutes, scraping bowl frequently. Pour into a greased tube or bundt pan and bake for 40 minutes in a 350 degree oven. Serve with whipped cream.

28

```
┌─────────────────────────────────────────────────┐
│                                                 │
│              WELSH RABBIT                       │
│                                                 │
│            WALDORF SALAD                         │
│                                                 │
│             CHESS CAKE                           │
│                                                 │
└─────────────────────────────────────────────────┘
```

WELSH RABBIT

1 lb. sharp processed Cheddar cheese	1/4 tsp. paprika
1½ cups heavy cream	8 English muffins, halved and toasted
2 tsp. Worcestershire sauce	16 slices fried bacon
1/2 tsp. mustard	16 tomato slices
1/4 tsp. cayenne	Parsley flakes

Melt cheese in double boiler. Add cream, Worcestershire sauce, mustard, cayenne, and paprika. Heat. To assemble: place hot muffin halves on each plate; tomato on each muffin half, 2 strips bacon over halves, cheese sauce, then parsley flakes. Serve.

WALDORF SALAD

8 cups chopped Red Delicious apples	1 cup English walnuts
2 cups celery	1/2 cup mayonnaise
	1/2 cup sour cream

Mix all ingredients together.

29

CHESS CAKE

1 cup butter	2 cups sifted flour
1 lb. light brown sugar	1 tsp. baking powder
1/2 cup white sugar	1 cup chopped pecans
4 eggs	1 tsp. vanilla

Heat butter and sugar over low heat. Add other ingredients in order given. Pour into a greased and floured 9 x 13 pan. Bake 40 to 50 minutes in a 300 degree oven. Cool 10 minutes. Cut in squares. Roll in confectioners sugar. Good served with vanilla ice cream on side.

MELANGE OF CHIPPED BEEF AND MUSHROOMS

OVER CHINESE NOODLES

CONGEALED BEET SALAD - SPOON ROLLS

FIVE FLAVOR POUND CAKE

MELANGE OF CHIPPED BEEF AND MUSHROOMS
OVER CHINESE NOODLES

2 cans cream of mush- room soup	1 8 oz. can mushroom pieces, drained
2 cans chicken and rice soup	1 8 oz. can water chest- nuts, sliced and
3 pkg. chipped beef 3 3 oz. cans Chinese noodles	drained

Combine ingredients except for Chinese noodles.
Heat and serve over warmed Chinese noodles.

CONGEALED BEET SALAD

1 6 oz. pkg. lemon gelatin	2 tbsp. horseradish 2tbsp. grated onion
2 cups hot water	1 16 oz. can diced beets
1/4 cup vinegar	with juice
1/2 tsp. salt	1 cup grated cucumber optional

Dissolve gelatin in hot water. Add other ingredients.
Congeal. Garnish with salad dressing.

SPOON ROLLS

1 pkg. dry yeast
2 tbsp. warm water (110°)
2 cups warm water
3/4 cup vegetable oil

4 cups self-rising flour
1/4 cup sugar
1 egg

Dissolve yeast in 2 tbsp. water. Combine all remaining ingredients. Spoon into greased muffin tins. Bake for 15 to 20 minutes in a 400 degree oven. The batter will keep in the refrigerator for several days so it may be made ahead of time and baked when needed.

FIVE FLAVOR CAKE

1 cup butter or
  margarine
1/2 cup vegetable
  shortening
3 cups sugar
5 eggs, well beaten
3 cups all purpose flour

1/2 tsp. baking powder
1 cup milk
1 tsp. coconut extract
1 tsp. rum extract
1 tsp. butter extract
1 tsp. lemon extract
1 tsp. vanilla extract

Cream butter, shortening and sugar until light and fluffy. Add eggs which have been beaten until lemon colored. Combine flour and baking powder. Add to cream mixture alternately with milk. Stir in flavorings. Spoon mixture into greased 10 inch tube pan and bake at 325 degrees for 1½ hours, or until cake tests done. Add glaze if desired or cool in pan about 10 minutes before turning out.

Glaze

1 cup sugar
1/2 cup water
1 tsp. coconut extract
1 tsp. butter extract

1 tsp. lemon extract
1 tsp. rum extract
1 tsp. vanilla extract

Combine and bring to boil. Pour over hot cake in pan. Let sit in pan until cool.

```
┌─────────────────────────────────────────────────────────┐
│                                                         │
│   HOT TUNA SANDWICH WITH MUSHROOM CHEESE SAUCE          │
│                                                         │
│               CORN RELISH                               │
│                                                         │
│               LEMON FREEZE                              │
│                                                         │
└─────────────────────────────────────────────────────────┘
```

HOT TUNA SANDWICH

2 7 oz. cans white tuna, drained	1/2 tsp. salt
1 can cream of mushroom soup	1 tsp. minced onion
6 hard boiled eggs, chopped	1/4 cup chopped pimento
1/4 cup salad dressing	1/2 cup chopped green pepper
	16 slices bread

Mix ingredients together. Spread between slices of
bread. Butter top and bottom of sandwiches. Place
in shallow pan. Bake 25 minutes in a 350 degree oven.
Serve with Mushroom Cheese Sauce.

MUSHROOM CHEESE SAUCE

1/2 cup butter	2 8 oz. cans mushroom pieces
1/2 cup flour	1 can mushroom soup
1/2 tsp. salt	1/2 lb. Cheddar cheese, grated
1/8 tsp. pepper	
4 cups milk	

Make a white sauce: heat butter. Add flour, salt and
pepper. When bubbly, add milk slowly, stirring constantly. Bring to a boil. Add remaining ingredients.
Heat until cheese melts.

CORN RELISH

4 cups frozen yellow
   corn
1½ cups grated cabbage
1/2 cup celery, diced
1 2 oz. jar pimento,
   chopped

1 tsp. salt
1 green pepper, chopped
1 onion, chopped
1/2 cup sugar
1 tbsp. dry mustard
1½ cups vinegar

Mix all ingredients. Bring to a boil and simmer 20 minutes. Cool. Refrigerate for 24 hours before serving.

LEMON FREEZE

1 15 oz. can evaporated
   milk, chilled
1 cup sugar
1/4 cup lemon juice

1/4 tsp. lemon extract
2 drops yellow food
   coloring

Line 9 x 9 pan with graham cracker crumbs. Whip well chilled evaporated milk until thick. Add sugar, lemon juice, lemon extract and yellow food coloring. Freeze. Cut in squares to serve. Garnish as desired.

```
┌─────────────────────────────────────────────┐
│                                             │
│           QUICHE LORRAINE                    │
│                                             │
│          FRESH FRUIT CUTS                    │
│                                             │
│         APRICOT NECTAR CAKE                  │
│                                             │
└─────────────────────────────────────────────┘
```

QUICHE LORRAINE

4 tbsp. butter	2 egg yolks
4 small onions, minced	2 eggs
1 tsp. salt	1½ cups light cream
1 tsp. pepper	1/8 tsp. nutmeg
6 slices bacon, fried	1 tsp. chopped chives
and crumbled	1 unbaked 9 inch pie
1 cup shredded Gruyere	crust
cheese	

Melt butter in pan; add onions; saute until onions
are soft. Season with salt and pepper. Drain onions
and put in bottom of pie crust. Add bacon. Sprinkle
with cheese. Beat together egg yolks, eggs, light
cream, nutmeg and chives. Pour into pie crust. Bake
for 30 minutes in a 350 degree oven. Let set about
5 minutes before cutting.

APRICOT NECTAR CAKE

1 box yellow or lemon	1 cup vegetable oil
cake mix	1 cup apricot nectar
1 3 oz. box lemon gelatin	6 eggs

Mix together in mixer and bake in ungreased 10
inch tube pan at 350 degrees for 50 minutes or
until done.

GLAZE FOR APRICOT NECTAR CAKE:

2 cups confectioners   1 cup orange juice
   sugar
1 lemon, juice and rind grated

Mix and pour over cake while in pan.

NOTES

REMEMBER - Each recipe serves 6 -8 unless otherwise
          stated.

```
┌─────────────────────────────────────────────────────────┐
│  GRANDMOTHER HUBBARD'S FROZEN FRUIT SALAD                │
│                                                          │
│      TEA PUNCH - FINGER SANDWICHES                       │
│                                                          │
│              CHESS PIE                                   │
│                                                          │
└─────────────────────────────────────────────────────────┘
```

GRANDMOTHER HUBBARD'S FROZEN FRUIT SALAD

1 can apricots, chopped	1 can mandarin oranges
1 can pears, chopped	2 bananas, sliced
1 bottle red cherry halves	1 cup pecans, chopped, optional
1 can crushed pineapple	

Drain fruits. Set aside. Prepare dressing:

2 eggs, beaten	1 small jar marshmallow cream
4 tbsp. vinegar	1 6 oz. carton whipped topping
4 tbsp. sugar	

Combine eggs, vinegar and sugar in heavy pan. Cook
until thick, stirring constantly. Remove from heat.
Cool. Add marshmallow cream and whipped topping.
Add fruit and mix well. Pour into individual molds.
Freeze for 24 hours. Garnish with Party Salad Topping
(page 58) and fresh strawberry.

PIMENTO CHEESE SANDWICH FILLING

1 lb. American Processed cheese	1/2 tsp. salt
3/4 cup mayonnaise	1/4 tsp. tabasco
1/2 jar pimentos, diced with juice	

Pimento Cheese Sandwich Filling (continued)

Grate cheese into mixing bowl. Add mayonnaise, pimento with juice, salt and tabasco. Mix well. Makes 2 2/3 cups.

TEA PUNCH

7 tea bags	2 6 oz. cans frozen
2 cups sugar	lemonade concentrate
2 6 oz. cans frozen	Enough water to finish
orange juice con-	1 gallon
centrate	Sprigs of fresh mint

Brew tea. Mix other ingredients. (You may add other juices such as peach, pear, pineapple, apricot. Remember to cut down on the amount of sugar when you add these sweetened juices.) Yield: 1 gallon. If extra juices are added you will have more than 1 gallon.

CHESS PIE

1/2 cup butter, melted	1 tsp. cornmeal
1 tbsp. vinegar	1½ cups sugar
3 eggs, beaten well	1 unbaked 9 inch pie
1 tsp. vanilla	crust
1 tsp. flour	

Combine ingredients and bake until brown in a 300 degree oven. Continue baking for 40 minutes in a 200 degree oven.

```
┌─────────────────────────────────────────────────────┐
│                                                     │
│           HAM AND YEAST ROLLS                       │
│                                                     │
│      CHEESE SOUFFLE - PINK ARTIC FREEZE             │
│                                                     │
│              DUMP CAKE                              │
│                                                     │
│                                                     │
└─────────────────────────────────────────────────────┘
```

CHEESE SOUFFLE

7 slices bread, crusts removed	1 tsp. Worcestershire sauce
2½ cups milk	8 oz. sharp cheese, grated
1 tsp. salt	3 eggs, separated
1/8 tsp. garlic powder	
1/8 tsp. cayenne	

Soak bread in milk, break into tiny bits. Add salt, garlic powder, cayenne, Worcestershire sauce and cheese. Beat egg yolks and whites separately; fold both into bread-cheese mixture. Put in a 2 quart buttered casserole. Start in cold oven. Bake for 1 hour at 350 degrees.

PINK ARTIC FREEZE

1 8 oz. pkg. cream cheese softened	1 cup crushed pineapple, drained
2 tbsp. mayonnaise	1 cup heavy cream, whipped
2 tbsp. sugar	
1 16 oz. can whole berry cranberry sauce	

Beat cream cheese, mayonnaise and sugar with electric mixer. Add cranberry sauce and pineapple. Mix well. Fold in whipped cream. Freeze in a 9 x 9 dish. Cut into squares to serve.

DUMP CAKE

1 20 oz. can crushed
 pineapple
1 3½ oz. can angel
 flake coconut
1 cup brown sugar

1 box yellow cake mix
1 cup butter
1 cup chopped nuts

Oil 13 x 9 pan. Dump can of pineapple with juice and spread over bottom of pan. Sprinkle coconut, then brown sugar, then yellow cake mix and spread evenly. Cut butter into thin slices and dot over cake. Sprinkle nuts over top. Bake in preheated 300 degree oven for 1 hour. Cut into squares and serve with vanilla ice cream. Serves 12 to 16.

```
+------------------------------------------------------------------+
|                                                                  |
|             SPLIT PEA SOUP WITH SHERRY                           |
|                                                                  |
|                 GREEN SALAD                                      |
|                                                                  |
|    PUMPKIN SQUARES WITH CREAM CHEESE FROSTING                    |
|                                                                  |
|                                                                  |
+------------------------------------------------------------------+
```

SPLIT PEA SOUP WITH SHERRY

1/4 cup butter	2 cups cooked ham, chopped
1/4 cup onion, chopped	2 cans split pea soup
1/4 cup celery, chopped	1½ cans milk
1/4 cup carrot, chopped	1/4 cup sherry

Saute onion, celery, carrot in butter. Add ham.
Simmer 10 minutes. Add remaining ingredients. Heat
and serve. Garnish with fresh snipped parsley.

PUMPKIN SQUARES

4 eggs	1/8 tsp. salt
2 cups sugar	2 tsp. baking soda
1 cup vegetable oil	2 tsp. cinnamon
2 cups flour	2 cups pumpkin pie filling

Mix together eggs, sugar, oil. Add sifted dry
ingredients. Blend in pumkin pie filling. Bake
in a greased 12 x 18 pan for 25 - 30 minutes in a
350 degree oven. Cut into squares to serve.

CREAM CHEESE FROSTING

1/2 cup soft butter
1 lb. box confectioners
   sugar
1 8 oz. pkg. soft cream
   cheese

1 tsp. vanilla
1 cup chopped walnuts

Mix and spread over cooled pumpkin cake.

NOTES

REMEMBER - Each recipe serves 6 - 8 people unless
       otherwise stated.

MISS DAISY AT HOME

The reasons for the success of Daisy's differ according to the teller, but there is no question that each one begins and ends with Daisy King. Her earliest memories of food date back to her grandparents' farm in Georgia where she learned first about food "Southern Style" from the garden to the table. After graduation from Belmont College, Daisy taught Home Economics in college and high schools in Nashville, did freelance work for a national grocery chain as a home economist, and finally, her catering with a friend led her into meeting Calvin and Marilyn Lahew. A partnership ensued and Miss Daisy's Restaurant became a reality for her.

At home, Daisy moves easily into the role of mother to two active boys and wife to Wayne King. The Kings enjoy entertaining in their home as well as dining out. And, like most good cooks, Daisy frequently tries new recipes on her own family, always looking for new and interesting ways to prepare and serve food. Although she is an extremely energetic, dynamic and optimistic person, Daisy makes it quite clear that loving, dedicated grandparents are the real stars behind the scenes because of their caring for her children while she works.

After the last restaurant guest leaves, you may find Daisy going home to work in her yard, finish a piece of needlepoint or read a cookbook. However, first and foremost, Daisy's hobby is people. Her bubbly personality and her astounding memory for names and faces indicate how very much Daisy enjoys meeting people. She believes every friendship is a special treasure.

Early in life Daisy was taught that every day is important. Her philosophy is simply to do your best each day and enjoy whatever the day brings. Whether at home, or at her restaurants, Daisy King is truly a remarkable lady.

A P P E T I Z E R S

HOT BROCCOLI DIP

1/2 cup butter
1 onion, chopped
1 can mushroom soup
1 4 oz. can chopped
  mushrooms

1 pkg. frozen chopped
  broccoli
1 roll of garlic cheese

Melt butter and saute onions until clear. Add soup,
mushrooms (with liquid) and cheese until it melts.
Add cooked broccoli. Serve hot with your favorite
crackers.

CHILI CON QUESO

1 lb. processed cheese
1 large can tomatoes,
  drained

1 can hot green chili
Onion juice

Melt cheese in double boiler. Add tomatoes and
green chili. Add a little onion juice to taste.
Serve with corn chips or crackers. Yield: 2-3 cups.

CRAB DIP DIVINE

1 12 oz. bottle catsup
1 12oz. bottle chili
  sauce
1/4 cup horseradish
Juice of 1 lemon

1/8 tsp. hot sauce
1/8 tsp. Worcestershire
  sauce
2 6½ oz. cans flaked
  crabmeat

Blend all ingredients together. Chill. Serve in pineapple shell with crip crackers. Yield: 3 cups.

45

CURRY DIP

1 pint salad dressing
1 garlic clove, crushed
3 tbsp. grated onion
1½ tbsp. Worcestershire
   sauce

5 tbsp. catsup
5 tbsp. curry powder
1 tbsp. salt
1 tsp. hot

Mix well. Refrigerate before serving.

GUACOMOLE DIP

4 ripe avocados
2 tsp. onion juice
2 ripe tomatoes, diced
   and drained

2 tsp. lemon juice
Salt
Cayenne pepper

Sieve avocado. Add remaining ingredients. Add
french dressing until desired consistency is
obtained.

SHRIMP DIP

1 8 oz. pkg. cream cheese
2 cups boiled shrimp,
   finely chopped
1 cup sour cream
1/2 tsp. salt

1/2 tsp. Worcestershire
   sauce
2 tsp. lemon juice
1/2 tsp. hot sauce

Combine all ingredients. Blend well. Refrigerate
several hours before serving.

SOUR CREAM AND ONION DIP

1 pint sour cream
1 envelope onion soup mix

Combine ingredients and serve with potato chips.

BLACK-EYED SUSANS

1/4 lb. sharp cheese,
  grated
1 cup butter
3 cups sifted flour

1/2 tsp. salt
Dates
Pecan halves

Combine cheese and butter until creamed. Add
salt to flour and mix with cheese and butter.
Take 1 tsp. mix, flatten. In middle of flattened
mix add date and wrap mix around date. Place
pecan half on top. Bake for 10-15 minutes on
ungreased baking sheet in pre-heated 450 degree
oven. Yield: 6 dozen.

CHEESE BALL

1 lb. Cheddar cheese
1 lb. cream cheese
1 grated onion

Worcestershire and hot
  sauce if desired

Grate or grind the Cheddar and mix well with
other ingredients. Form into a ball. Roll in
chopped parsley or walnuts.

CHEESE STRAWS

1/4 lb. Cheddar cheese,
  grated
1 cup flour

1/2 cup butter
1/8 tsp. salt
1/8 tsp. paprika

Mix together thoroughly. Roll or cut into straw
shapes. Bake 12 minutes in a 350 degree oven.
Yield: 3 dozen.

CUCUMBER BALL

1 large pkg. cream
  cheese
1 large cucumber,
  chopped
2 tsp. mayonnaise

1/2 small onion, grated
1/8 tsp. hot sauce
1/8 tsp. Worcestershire
  sauce

Form a ball, wrap in foil and refrigerate.

POPPY SEED SQUARES

1 lb. Cheddar cheese
1 cup butter, softened

Poppy seed
5 dozen toast squares

Cream cheese and butter well. Spread on toast
squares. Sprinkle with poppy seeds and heat in a
350 degree oven until toasted. Yield 5 dozen.

MARINATED MUSHROOMS

120 fresh button
  mushrooms
20 lemons (5 cups juice)

2½ cups olive oil
Salt and pepper

Wash and peel mushrooms. Place 24 mushrooms per
shallow dish and pour the juice of 4 lemons and
1/2 cup olive oil over them. Marinate for at least
2 hours. Drain and serve with individual colored
cocktail picks. Yield: 120 each.

STUFFED MUSHROOMS

1 tbsp. oil
1 tbsp. butter
1 tbsp. minced onion
2 tbsp. dry bread crumbs

Salt and pepper to taste
Milk
Mushrooms

Wash and wipe mushrooms carefully. Remove centers
and stems. Heat oil and butter in heavy skillet.
Place mushrooms in skillet, hollow side up, season
with salt and pepper. Cook over medium heat 10
minutes. Drain on toweling. Saute onion, chopped
stems and centers in butter about 5 minutes. Add
dry bread crumbs, salt and pepper and just enough
milk to moisten. Fill mushroom caps with stuffing,
of thyme, covered and refrigerated until ready to
serve. Heat 15 minutes in a 350 degree oven.
Yield: 3 dozen.

TOASTED MUSHROOM ROLLS

2 lbs. fresh mushrooms,
   diced
1 cup butter
3/4 cup flour
1 tsp. Accent seasoning
1 tbsp. salt
4 cups light cream
2½ tbsp. chives, minced
4 tsp. lemon juice
4 sandwich loaves of
   white bread, trimmed

Peel mushrooms and dice. Saute for 5 minutes in
butter. Blend in flour, Accent and salt. Stir in
light cream and simmer until thick. Add minced
chives and lemon juice. Blend well. Remove crusts
from bread and roll slices thin. Spread with mixture and roll up. Cut in half and toast on all
sides about 20 minutes in a 400 degree oven. These
are true delicacies and can be made far in advance
to freeze for future use. If you plan to freeze,
don't toast until ready to serve. Yield: 13 dozen.

NUTS AND BOLTS

1 16 oz. can mixed nuts
4 tsp. garlic salt
4 tsp. celery salt
4 tsp. Worcestershire
   sauce
2 tsp. hot sauce
3/4 cup butter, melted
1 box each:
   Corn Chex
   Wheat Chex
   Rice Chex
   Cheese Nips
   Pretzels

Blend together thoroughly melted butter, garlic
salt, celery salt, Worcestershire sauce and hot
sauce. Combine dry ingredients in a pan and add
butter mixture. Mix well and bake for 2 hours at
200 degrees, stirring every 15 minutes.

PEPPERY SPICED NUTS

2 tbsp. butter, melted
1 lb. pecan or walnut
  halves
2 tsp. Worcestershire
  sauce

1/8 tsp. hot sauce
1/2 tsp. salt
1/4 tsp. pepper

In skillet saute pecan or walnut halves in butter until hot. Add remaining ingredients. Arrange nuts in shallow pan and bake for 20 minutes at 325 degrees. Yield: 4 cups.

SMOKED TURKEY FINGERS

100 thin slices smoked turkey
1 8 oz. pkg. cream cheese

Spread thin slices of smoked turkey with cream cheese. Roll up each slice. Sprinkle with paprika and serve. Yield: 100. Use turkey, beef, or corned beef in packages for this.

BEVERAGES

HOT SPICED APPLE CIDER

9 46 oz. cans apple
  juice
2 tsp. cinnamon

2 tsp. nutmeg
2 tsp. allspice
2 tsp. ground cloves

Blend all ingredients together and heat thoroughly.
Yield: 100 4 oz. servings.

HOT CHOCOLATE MIX

2 lb. box instant
  chocolate drink mix
1 lb. box confectioners
  sugar

11 oz. jar powdered
  creamer
8 quart box powdered
  milk

Mix together and sift. Store in jars. Fill cup half
full of mix and finish filling with hot water.
Makes a nice gift.

COCA-COLA PUNCH

12 lemons, juiced
3 cups sugar

5 pints water
6 king size Coca-Colas

Combine lemon juice, sugar and water. Let stand overnight in refrigerator. When ready to serve add Coca-
Colas and ice. Good punch for children. Yield: 25
punch cup servings.

CRAN-ORANGE PUNCH

1 gallon cranberry juice
1 gallon orange juice

Mix juice and serve over ice cubes. A spring
of fresh mint completes this beverage. Yield:
2 gallons.

HOT CRANBERRY TEA

1 quart cranberry juice   2 cups water
Scant 1/2 cup candy red   Juice of 2 oranges
  hots   Juice of 2 lemons
2 cups sugar   Red food coloring

Combine cranberry juice and red hots in saucepan.
Heat slowly and stir until red hots dissolve. Add
sugar and water and heat until sugar dissolves.
Add juice of oranges and lemons. Dilute with water
to suit taste. Add red food coloring to desired
color. Yield: 15 servings.

HOT SPICED TEA

2 cups orange flavor   1/2 cup instant tea
  instant breakfast drink 1 tsp. cinnamon
1 cup sugar   1 tsp. ground cloves
1 10 oz. pkg. dry
  lemonade mix

Mix ingredients. Keep covered in glass jar. Use
1-2 teaspoons per cup of water.

SANGRIA

1/2 lb. strawberries, washed and halved
2 ripe peaches, peeled and cut into small pieces
1 orange, thinly sliced

1 lime, thinly sliced
Juice and rind of 1 lemon
1/2 cup sugar
3/4 tsp. cinnamon
2 bottles red wine

Put all ingredients in pitcher, add wine and stir thoroughly, mashing the fruit slightly. Let stand at room temperature for at least 1 hour. Just before serving, add 20 ice cubes and stir until cold.

HOT V-8

Use equal parts of V-8 juice and beef bouillon. Add celery salt, hot sauce and Worcestershire sauce to taste, and heat thoroughly.

S A L A D S

APRICOT SALAD

1 6 oz. pkg. apricot   2 large cans apricots
  gelatin   1 pint sour cream
1 envelope plain gelatin
1 large can crushed pineapple

Dissolve apricot gelatin in 3 cups hot juice from
cans of pineapple and apricots, mix with apricots,
pineapple and sour cream. Add to cool gelatin. Mix
and pour into molds. Yield: 24 servings.

BING CHERRY SALAD

2 3 oz. pkg. black   1 cup celery, finely
  cherry gelatin   chopped
3 cups boiling water   2 tbsp. lemon juice
Juice drained from cherries 1 cup pecans, finely
  plus water to make 1 cup   chopped
  liquid
1 can Bing cherries, drained

Dissolve gelatin in boiling water. Add juice-
water mixture. Add remaining ingredients. Chill
until firm. Salad may be frozen if desired.
Yield: 12 servings.

CONGEALED GREEN PEA SALAD

1 3 oz. pkg. lemon
  gelatin
1 3/4 cups hot water
1/2 cup nuts

1 cup small green peas,
  drained
1 cup chopped celery
1 cup sliced green olives

Dissolve gelatin in hot water. Cool and when it
begins to thicken, add other ingredients and mold.
Serve with mayonnaise on lettuce.

BLACK-EYED PEA SALAD-GREEK STYLE

4 15 oz. cans black-eyed
  peas, drained
1 cup diced celery
1 cup scallions (include
  2-3 inch of green ends)
  chopped
1/4 tsp. (scant) garlic
  powder

1/2 tsp. oregano leaves
  crushed between palms
1/4 cup plus 2 tbsp. oil
1/4 cup plus 2 tbsp.
  vinegar

Mix all ingredients well. Marinate, stirring
occsionally, overnight

PINEAPPLE SALAD SUPREME

2 tbsp. gelatin
1 large can crushed
  pineapple
1 pint cottage cheese
1 chopped green pepper
1/2 cup chopped pimento

1/2 cup cold water
1 tbsp. sugar
3/4 cup salad dressing
1/2 pint heavy cream,
  whipped
1 cup nuts

Dissolve gelatin in cold water, heat over hot water
to liquid consistency. Add gelatin to all other ingredients combined. Congeal.

PEPPERMINT STICK CANDY SALAD

1 3 oz. pkg. lime
  gelatin
1 cup hot water
3/4 cup pineapple juice
1/2 pint heavy cream,
  whipped

1 medium can crushed
  pineapple
3/4 cup pecans, chopped
6 sticks peppermint
  candy, crushed

Dissolve gelatin in hot water. Add pineapple juice.
Chill until firm. then beat until fluffy. Next,
fold in 1/2 pint whipped cream. Complete by adding
pineapple, nuts and 3 sticks crushed candy. Chill
until ready to serve. Sprinkle remaining 3 sticks
of crushed candy on top of salad. Serves 8-10.

SEVEN CUP SALAD

1 cup grated coconut
1 cup cottage cheese
1 cup sour cream
1 cup chopped nuts

1 cup crushed pineapple
1 cup fruit cocktail
1 cup miniature marsh-
  mallows

Combine all ingredients and put in refrigerator.
This salad improves after it sets a day or two.

ORANGE SHERBERT SALAD

1 6 oz. pkg. orange
  gelatin
2 cups boiling water
1 pint orange sherbert
1 11 oz. can mandarin oranges

2 bananas, sliced
1 small can crushed
  pineapple

Dissolve gelatin in 2 cups boiling water, add
sherbert, stir until dissolved. Add remaining
ingredients. Let stand until congealed in
refrigerator.

SUMMER SALAD

1 3 oz. pkg. lime gelatin
2 cups miniature marshmallows
1 small pkg. cream cheese
1/2 pint heavy cream
1 cup hot water
1 small can crushed pineapple
1/2 cup chopped pecans

Dissolve gelatin in hot water; when it begins to thicken, add marshmallows and other ingredients. Whip cream before adding to mixture. Chill. Serve on lettuce.

PARTY SALAD TOPPING

1 4½ oz. carton whipped topping
1/4 cup salad dressing
1/4 cup instant breakfast orange drink mix

Mix well. Refrigerate until serving time.

NOTES

REMEMBER – Each recipe serves 6 – 8 people unless otherwise noted.

VEGETABLES

BEST BAKED BEANS

6 slices bacon
2 green peppers,
  chopped fine
1 small onion,
  chopped fine
1/2 cup brown sugar

1/2 cup catsup
1 tsp. mustard
1 tsp. Worcestershire
  sauce
1 large can pork and
  beans

Combine all ingredients, arrange bacon across top of mixture. Bake uncovered 1½ - 2 hours in a 325 degree oven.

GREEN BEAN CASSEROLE

1 can French green beans
  or 1 pkg. frozen beans
  cooked
1/2 onion, chopped
5-6 stalks celery, chopped
1 can cream of chicken
  soup

1 can bean spouts
1 can water chestnuts
  sliced thin
Grated cheese to cover
  top of casserole
1 can French fried
  onion rings

Place in casserole layers of vegetables, soup and water chestnuts. Sprinkle top with cheese and onion rings. Bake for 30 minutes in a 350 degree oven.

BROCCOLI WITH HORSERADISH DRESSING

1 pkg. frozen broccoli   1/2 cup water
1/4 tsp. salt

Bring water and salt to boil. Add frozen broccoli.
When second boil has been reached, turn to low and
cool 5 to 8 minutes. Blend:

1/2 cup salad dressing   2 tbsp. horseradish
1 tsp. sugar   mustard

Put generous helping of dressing on each serving
of broccoli.

BAKED LIMAS WITH SOUR CREAM

1 lb. dried limas   1 tbsp. dry mustard
3 tsp. salt   1 tbsp. molasses
1/2 cup margarine   1 cup sour cream
3/4 cup brown sugar

Soak beans overnight in water. Next morning drain
and cover with fresh water. Add 1 tsp. salt and
cook until tender 30-45 minutes. Drain again and
rinse under hot water. Put in casserole and dot
margarine over beans. Mix brown sugar, dry mustard
and rest of salt in bowl and sprinkle over beans.
Stir in molasses and finally pour over bean mixture the sour cream and mix tenderly. Bake for 60
minutes in a 350 degree oven.

EGGPLANT SOUFFLE

2 cups diced, peeled
   eggplant
1 cup bread crumbs
1 cup milk
1½ tsp. onion

2 tbsp. butter
1 cup grated cheese
3 eggs, beaten
1 tsp. black. pepper
1 tsp. salt

Soak eggplant in salt water for 1 hour. Drain well and cook until done. Mash eggplant and add remaining ingredients. Pour into buttered casserole and bake for 30-45 minutes in a 350 degree oven.

ONION CASSEROLE

4 cups sliced onion,
   cooked in salted water
   until tender, drained
1 can cream of mushroom
   soup

1/2 cup slivered almonds
1/3 cup melted butter
1 cup cornflake crumbs

Mix all ingredients together, topping with almonds. Bake until bubbly hot in a 350-375 degree oven.

PARTY SQUASH

1 lb. yellow squash
   sliced
1 tsp. sugar
1/2 cup mayonnaise
1/2 cup minced onion
1/4 cup finely chopped
   green pepper

1/2 cup chopped pecans
1 egg, slightly beaten
1/2 cup grated Cheddar
   cheese
Salt and pepper to taste
Bread or cracker crumbs
1/4 cup butter

Cook squash, drain and mash. Add other ingredients except butter and crumbs. Put in 2 quart casserole, top with crumbs, dot with butter. Bake for 35-40 minutes in a 350 degree oven.

SPINACH AND ARTICHOKE CASSEROLE

4 tbsp. garlic French salad dressing	3 tbsp. flour
2 cans artichoke hearts	1/4 tsp. salt
3 pkgs. frozen chopped spinach	1½ cups milk
3 tbsp. butter	1 tbsp. Parmesan cheese

Marinate artichokes in dressing for several hours. Saving dressing, drain artichokes and put in greased 2 quart casserole. Cook spinach as directed, drain. Make white sauce: melt butter in skillet; add flour cook until bubbly; add milk and salt; cook until it thickens, stirring constantly. Mix with spinach and reserved dressing. Pour over artichokes, top with cheese. Bake for 20 minutes in a 375 degree oven.

VEGETABLE CASSEROLE

1 small cauliflower	4 tbsp. flour
8 small potatoes	2 cups milk
8 small carrots	1 tsp. salt
10 small onions	1 tsp. pepper
1 cup canned or frozen green peas	1/2 lb. sharp cheese, grated
4 tbsp. butter	

Separate cauliflower into flowerets. Add next 3 ingredients; cook until tender. Drain well. Add drained peas. Put in 2 quart casserole. Make white sauce: melt butter in skillet; add flour; cook until bubbly; add milk, salt and pepper; cook until it thickens, stirring constantly. Add cheese, stir until melted. Pour over vegetables. Bake uncovered in a 375 degree oven to lightly brown sauce.

SWEET POTATOES IN ORANGE CUPS

3 cups cooked mashed   1/4 cup butter
  sweet potatoes   1/2 cup milk
1 cup sugar   1 tsp. vanilla
1/2 tsp. salt   Orange half shells
2 eggs

Mix all ingredients together and pour into
orange halves which have the pulp removed. Cover
with topping:

1 cup brown sugar   1 cup chopped nuts
1/3 cup flour   1/4 cup butter

Mix thoroughly and sprinkle over potato mixture
in orange cups. Bake 35 minutes in a 350 degree
oven.

HERBED TOMATOES

6 large ripe tomatoes   1/4 cup fresh or frozen
1 tsp. salt   chives
1/4 tsp. black pepper   2/3 cup salad oil
1/4 cup finely snipped   1/4 cup tarragon vinegar
  parsley

Peel tomatoes, cut crosswise in half. Place in deep
bowl, sprinkling each layer with seasonings and
herbs. Combine oil and vinegar and pour over tomatoes.
Cover, chill an hour or more, basting often. Drain
off dressing and arrange tomatoes on platter.
Yield: 12 servings.

BEEF BURGUNDY

2 to 3 medium onions, sliced	Thyme
2 tbsp. butter	Salt
2 lbs. lean beef, cut in 1½ x ½ inch strips	1/2 cup beef bouillon
	1 cup Burgundy wine
1½ tbsp. flour	Pepper
Marjoram	1/2 lb. sliced mushrooms

Saute onions in butter. Remove to separate dish.
Saute meat in same butter; brown. Sprinkle with
flour, marjoram, thyme, salt and pepper. Add
bouillon and Burgundy. Stir well. Cover and simmer
3 hours. The liquid seldom cooks away, but if it
seems dry, add more bouillon and wine. Add onions
and mushrooms. Stir well. Cook 1 hour longer.

CHICKEN BREASTS IN WINE

1/2 cup melted butter	1 cup heavy cream
Green onion, chopped	1 cup fresh mushrooms
4 chicken breasts, split	1 tsp. paprika
Salt and pepper to taste	Sliced ripe olives
1/2 cup Marsala wine	

In a skillet, saute green onion in butter. Add
chicken and cook until meat is lightly brown.
Add wine, cream, mushrooms, paprika and olives.
Cook covered until chicken is tender, approximately
20 minutes.

HOT BAKED CHICKEN SALAD

2 cups chopped cooked
  chicken
2 cups chopped celery
1/2 cup chopped pecans
1 cup salad dressing

1/2 tsp. salt
2 tbsp. lemon juice
2 tsp. minced onions
1/2 cup grated cheese
1 cup potato chips

Combine chicken, celery, nuts salad dressing, salt, lemon juice and onions. Pour into greased casserole dish. Mix remaining ingredients; sprinkle over casserole. Bake for 10 minutes in a 350 degree oven.

HAM CASSEROLE

1 can cream of mushroom
  soup
1 can green asparagus
2 cups chopped ham
1/4 cup grated cheese
2 tbsp. chopped onions

2 tbsp. green pepper
1 tbsp. lemon juice
2 tbsp. uncooked tapioca
1/2 cup light cream
Buttered bread crumbs

Arrange layers of ham and asparagus in a 2 quart casserole dish. Mix remaining ingredients except bread crumbs, and pour over ham and asparagus. Top with buttered bread crumbs. Bake for 30 minutes in a 375 degree oven.

CREOLE PORK CHOPS

6 center cut chops	1 green pepper
1 16 oz. can tomatoes	1/2 cup mushrooms
1 8 oz. can tomato sauce	1/4 cup water
1 small onion	Cooked rice

Brown chops which have been dredged in seasoned flour, salt, pepper, paprika in oil. Place in a 2 quart casserole dish. Add remaining ingredients except rice. Cover. Bake for 1½ - 2 hours in a 325 degree oven. Serve pork chops and sauce with rice which has been prepared according to directions on package.

FRENCH POT ROAST

1/4 lb. beef roast, rump	1 stalk celery, diced
1 clove garlic	1 sprig parsley
1/4 tsp. pepper	1 bay leaf
1 tsp. salt	1 sprig thyme
2 onions sliced	2 cups red wine (dry)
3 tbsp. bacon drippings	1 cup tomato puree
2 carrots, sliced	

Rub roast with garlic, pepper and salt. Brown onions in bacon drippings. Remove and brown roast on all sides. Add vegetables and brown. Add parsley, bay leaf, thyme, wine and tomato puree. Cover and bake for 3½ hours in a 350 degree oven. Add small amount of hot water during baking if needed.

STEAK ORIENTAL

2 lb. lean steak, 1¼-1½ inches thick, cut in thin slices
Meat tenderizer
1 tbsp. salad oil
1 tbsp. gravy sauce
1 tsp. salt
2 tbsp. soy sauce
3 beef bouillon cubes in 1 cup water
1 large onion, sliced thin
2 cups celery, cut in long thin strips
1 8 oz. pkg. frozen Chinese pea pods
1 tbsp. cornstarch in 2 tbsp. water
2 small red tomatoes, cut in wedges
4½ cups hot, fluffy rice with snipped parsley

Prepare meat with tenderizer according to directions on bottle. To hot salad oil and gravy sauce, add meat, stirring until brown. Add salt, soy sauce and bouillon. Simmer, covered 30 minutes or until fork tender. Add onion and celery on top of steak and cook over medium heat for 5 minutes. Add thawed pea pods, cook two minutes. Thicken liquid around steak with cornstarch mixture. Add tomato wedges. Remove from heat. Serve with hot rice.

TUNA CASHEW CASSEROLE

1 3 oz. can chow mein noodles
1 can cream of mushroom soup
1/4 cup water
1 6½ oz. can tuna
1 cup diced celery
1/4 cup chopped ripe olives
1/4 cup minced onion
1/2 tsp. salt
1/2 tsp. pepper
1/4 cup chopped cashews

Reserve 1 cup noodles, combine other ingredients. Pour into 1½ quart greased casserole dish. Sprinkle with reserved noodles and cashews just before baking. Bake 40 minutes in a 350 degree oven. Yield: 4-6 servings.

PARMESAN ROUND STEAK

1½ lb. round steak cut
  3/4 inches thick
1 tbsp. Accent seasoning
1 egg, beaten
1/3 cup milk
1/2 cup fine dry bread
  crumbs
Salt

1/8 tsp. pepper
3 tbsp. bacon drippings
1/2 cup water
1/4 tsp. leaf oregano
1/4 cup grated Parmesan
  cheese
1/4 tsp. paprika
6 small onions

Cut steak into 6 serving pieces. Pound to 1/2 inch thickness. Combine egg and milk. Mix bread crumbs, 1 tsp. salt, pepper and Accent. Dip steaks in egg mixture, dredge with seasoned crumbs. Brown meat in drippings, add water. Sprinkle oregano on steaks. Place 2 tsp. Parmesan cheese on each steak. Combine 1/4 tsp. salt and paprika. Sprinkle onions with salt mixture. Add to meat, cover tightly. Bake for 1½ to 2 hours in a 325 degree oven.

SAUSAGE CASSEROLE

1 lb. ground pork
  sausage
2 envelopes chicken
  noodle soup
1/2 cup uncooked rice
4½ cups boiling water

1 chopped green pepper
1 chopped medium onion
1/2 cup chopped celery
1/2 cup slivered almonds

Brown sausage, drain and set aside. In covered saucepan cook soup mix, rice and water 7 minutes. Then combine all ingredients and place in baking dish. (May be prepared day before needed) Bake 1 hour in 350 degree oven. Yield: 8-10 servings. Good served with mushroom gravy.

SEAFOOD AND RICE CASSEROLE

1 cup salad dressing
1¼ cups cooked rice
1 cup canned crabmeat
1 cup canned shrimp
1 small can mushrooms
5 tbsp. chopped onion
3 tbsp. Worcestershire
  sauce
1 chopped green pepper
Salt and pepper
Slivered almonds

Add salad dressing to rice while hot. Combine with other ingredients and place in casserole. 'Top with slivered almonds. Baked 30 minutes in a 350 degree oven. This can be made ahead and frozen, but allow to come to room temperature before baking.
Yield: 6 servings.

VEAL PARMESAN

1 lb. thinly sliced veal
2 eggs, beaten
1 cup bread crumbs
1/4 cup cooking oil
1 can condensed tomato
  soup
1/2 soup can water
1/4 cup minced onion
1 clove garlic, minced
1/8 tsp. thyme
4 oz. Mozzarella cheese
  thinly sliced
Grated Parmesan cheese

Cut veal into serving pieces. Dip into eggs then into bread crumbs. Brown veal in hot oil in skillet. Place in baking dish. Add soup, water, onion, garlic and thyme. Cook for 1½ hours in a 350 degree oven. Top with Mozzarella cheese, sprinkle with grated Parmesan cheese. Broil until cheese melts.

CHEESE DROP BISCUITS

2 cups sharp cheese,
  grated
1/4 cup shortening
2 eggs, well beaten
2 cups flour, sifted

3 tbsp. baking powder
1 tbsp. salt
1/4 tsp. cayenne pepper
1/2 cup water

Mix cheese, shortening and eggs. Add remaining ingredients, blending thoroughly. Drop onto greased cookie sheet. Biscuits should be the size of small walnuts. Bake about 15 minutes or until golden brown in a 425 degree oven. Yield: 5 dozen.

CHOCOLATE DATE BREAD

4 cups flour, sifted
2½ tbsp. baking powder
2 tsp. salt
1 cup sugar
1 cup chopped dates

2 cups strong coffee
1/4 tsp. soda
2 eggs, well beaten
1/4 cup vegetable oil
2 6 oz. pkgs. semi-sweet
  chocolate morsels

Preheat oven to 375 degrees. Grease and flour 9 x 5 x 3 pan. Into large bowl sift together flour, baking powder, salt and sugar. Add dates and chocolate chips. Blend together well. Stir in coffee, soda, eggs and vegetable oil. Pour into greased pan. Bake for 1 hour in a 375 degree oven.

QUICK LIGHT BREAD

1 cup boiling water
1/2 tsp. salt
2 tbsp. shortening
1/4 cup sugar
1/4 cup lukewarm water

1 tsp. sugar
1 pkg. dry yeast
4 cups flour
1 egg

Mix first 4 ingredients. Cool to lukewarm. Dissolve yeast in 1/4 cup lukewarm water and 1 tsp. sugar. Combine mixture, add egg and 2 cups flour, beat well, add remaining flour until moistened. Don't knead. Let rise until double in bulk, about 1 hour. Make into rolls or loaf. Place in a warm place about 1 hour to rise. Bake for 15-20 minutes for rolls or 25-30 minutes for loaf in a 425 degree oven.

CORN LIGHT BREAD

2 cups meal
3/4 cups sugar
1/2 cup flour
1/4 tsp. soda

3 tbsp. shortening,
  melted
2 cups buttermilk
1 tsp. salt

Mix dry ingredients with buttermilk and melted shortening. Bake in greased loaf pan until golden brown for 1 hour in a 350 degree oven. Turn on rack and cool.

PARMESAN CHEESE BISCUITS

1 can refrigerated
  biscuits

1/2 cup butter, melted
Parmesan cheese

Dip biscuits in butter and sprinkle with Parmesan. Stack in a slanted position, biscuits touching, in a loaf pan. Bake according to directions on can of biscuits.

CRANBERRY TEA BREAD

3 cups flour
1 tsp. salt
1/2 tsp. soda
3 tsp. baking powder
1/2 cup margarine, melted
1½ cups sugar
2 eggs

3/4 cup water
1/2 cup orange juice
1 tsp. grated orange rind
1 cup chopped nuts
1½ cup cranberries, cut
   in halves or coarsely
   chopped

Sift together flour, salt, soda, and baking powder.
Cream margarine and sugar. Add eggs and mix well.
Combine water, orange juice and rind and add alternately with sifted dry ingredients. Fold in nuts
and cranberries. Pour into a greased 9 x 5 loaf pan.
Bake for 1 hour in a 350 degree oven. Turn out onto
rack to cool. This bread slices better the second
day and freezes so well it can be made weeks ahead.

HELEN CORBITTS' LEMON MUFFINS

1 cup butter
1 cup sugar
4 egg yolks, well beaten
1/2 cup lemon juice
2 cups flour

2 tsp. baking powder
1 tsp. salt
4 egg whites, stiffly
   beaten
2 tsp. grated lemon peel

Cream butter and sugar until smooth. Add egg yolks
and beat until light. Add the lemon juice alternately with flour which has been sifted with baking
powder and salt, mixing thoroughly after each
addition. Fold in stiffly beaten egg whites and
grated lemon peel. Fill buttered muffin pans full
and bake about 20 minutes at 375 degrees. These
freeze well and are split and toasted with salads.

FUDGE MUFFINS

4 blocks semi-sweet
  chocolate
1 cup melted margarine
1/2 tsp. salt
1 cup sugar

1 cup flour
4 eggs
1 tsp. vanilla
2 cups chopped walnuts

Melt margarine and chocolate in pan. Beat in sugar, salt and flour. Then add eggs one at a time, stirring in. Add vanilla and chopped walnuts. Pour into a greased 24-cup muffin pan and bake for 25 minutes at 325 degrees.

TROPICAL MUFFINS

1 3/4 cups sifted flour
1/2 cup sugar
2 tsp. baking powder
1/4 tsp. soda
3/4 tsp. salt
1/3 cup orange juice
1/2 cup coconut

1/3 cup shortening
  melted
1 egg, beaten
1 cup ripe bananas,
  mashed
1 tsp. orange rind

Sift dry ingredients together. Add coconut. Combine shortening, egg, banana, orange juice and rind. Add to dry ingredients. Stir quickly with a fork only until dry ingredients are moistened. Bake for 25-30 minutes in a 375 degree oven. Yield: 12-18 muffins.

PINEAPPLE SURPRISE

1/2 cup margarine
3 eggs, beaten
1/2 cup sugar

1 16 oz. can crushed
  pineapple
5 slices bread, cubed

Mix first 4 ingredients and stir into bread cubes. Bake in a covered casserole for 40 minutes in a 350 degree oven. Cut in squares. This is especially good with ham.

REFRIGERATOR POTATO ROLLS

1 cake yeast
1/2 cup lukewarm water
2/3 cup shortening
1/2 cup sugar
1 tsp. salt

1 cup Irish potatoes,
 potatoes
1 cup milk, scalded
2 eggs, well beaten
5½-6 cups flour, sifted

Dissolve yeast in lukewarm water. Mix shortening, sugar, salt and mashed potatoes. Add scalded milk. Cool to room temperature. Add yeast and eggs. Gradually add flour and mix well. Form to desired number of rolls and let rise to double bulk. Bake for 15-20 minutes in a 400 degree oven. Cover and refrigerate remaining dough. Use as needed. Let rise before baking. Yield: 5 dozen rolls.

NOTES

REMEMBER - Each recipe serves 6 - 8 people unless otherwise stated.

APPLE CRISP

4 cups sliced tart apples
1/2 cup water
2 tbsp. lemon juice
1 tsp. cinnamon

3/4 cup flour
1/2 cup butter
1 cup white or brown
  sugar

Arrange apples in buttered baking dish. Pour over
water. Blend flour, sugar, cinnamon and butter with
pastry blender. Place this mixture on top of apples.
Bake for 30 minutes in a 350 degree oven. Serve
warm with ice cream.

CHOCOLATE TARTS

2 cups milk
2 squares unsweetened
  chocolate
1 cup sugar
1/3 cup flour

1/2 tsp. salt
3 egg yolks
1 tbsp. butter
1 tsp. vanilla

Melt chocolate and milk over low heat. Add enough
milk mixture to make a paste of sugar, flour and
salt. Slowly add this mixture back to chocolate
and milk mixture. Cook over low heat to medium
heat, continuously stirring, until thick. Beat 3
egg yolks and slowly add to mixture. Cook slowly 1
minute, then add butter and vanilla. Cool and fill
cooked tart shells. This recipe makes a delicious
chocolate pie.

CREME DE MENTHE PARTY DESSERT

55 large marshmallows
1 cup real creme de menthe

2 cups heavy cream
40 double lady fingers

Dissolve marshmallows in creme de menthe in top of double boiler. Let cool. Beat cream and fold into mixture. Line two 8 inch square pans with cross pieces of wax paper. Line sides and bottom with opened lady fingers. Alternate lady fingers with creme de menthe mixture. Creme de menthe mixture should be last layer on top. Put whipped cream on top and sprinkle with shaved bitter chocolate. Lift from pan with wax paper. Refrigerate. Yield: 18 servings.

FAT MAN'S MISERY

14 chocolate cream
  cookies
1/2 cup butter
1 cup confectioners
  sugar
1 egg

Few drops almond flavoring
2 cups heavy cream
1/2 tbsp. sugar
1 tsp. vanilla
1 cup chopped pecans

Crush cookies. Line 9 inch pie pan or square pan with most of the crushed cookies, saving some for topping. Cream butter and sugar. Add egg, cream again. Add almond flavoring. Spread this mixture on crumbs. Whip cream with sugar. Add vanilla and pecans. Fold until well blended. Spread this on first mixture. Cover with crushed cookies. Let stand in refrigerator for 24 hours.

HELLO DOLLIES

1/2 cup butter, melted
1 cup finely crushed graham cracker crumbs

Mix above and place in 9 inch square pan. Place the
following in pan in order given:

1 cup flaked coconut   1 cup chopped nuts
1 cup chocolate morsels

Pour 1 can sweetened condensed milk over mixture
and smooth out evenly. Bake for 25-30 minutes at
350 degrees. Let cool in pan and cut in small
squares because these are very rich.

PEACH COBBLER

2 cups sliced fresh   3/4 cup flour
  peaches   2 tsp. baking powder
2 cups sugar   1/4 tsp. salt
1/2 cup butter   3/4 cup milk

Mix peaches with 1 cup sugar. Let stand. Put butter
in a 2 quart casserole, place in a 325 degree oven
to melt. Combine remaining sugar, flour, baking
powder, salt and milk. Pour over melted butter.
Do not stir. Spoon peaches on top of batter. Do
not stir. Bake for 1 hour in a 325 degree oven.
You can use canned peaches.

LEMON SQUARES

1 cup flour   1/2 cup butter
1/4 cup confectioners sugar

Cream above ingredients and press evenly in bottom
of 9 inch square pan. Bake 20 minutes at 350
degrees. Beat together the following:

1 cup sugar   2 eggs
1/2 tsp. salt   4 tbsp. lemon juice
1 tsp. baking powder

Pour above ingredients over hot crust and bake 20 -
25 minutes at 350 degrees until no imprint remains
when touched lightly. Cool and cut into 2 inch squares.
You may want to sprinkle with confectioners sugar.

NOTES

REMEMBER - Each recipe serves 6 - 8 people unless
         otherwise stated.

FRESH APPLE CAKE

1½ cups salad oil
2 cups sugar
3 eggs
2½ cups flour
2 tsp. baking powder
3 cups chopped tart apples

1 tsp. salt
1 tsp. soda
1 cups nuts (I use walnuts)
1 tsp. vanilla

Cream first three ingredients together. Sift dry ingredients and mix gradually into creamed mixture. Fold in nuts, vanilla and apples. Bake in a tube pan for 1 hour in a 350 degree oven or in two loaf pans for 1 hour in a 300 degree oven. Reduce heat to 250 degrees until done.

KENTUCKY BUTTER CAKE

3 cups sifted cake flour
1 tsp. baking powder
1 tsp. salt
1/2 tsp soda
2 cups sugar

4 eggs, unbeaten
1 cup buttermilk
2 tsp. rum flavoring
1 cup butter

Sift dry ingredients together. Cream well butter and sugar. Blend in unbeaten eggs one at a time, beating well after each addition. Combine buttermilk and rum flavoring. Add alternately with dry ingredients. Blend well after each addition. Turn into tube pan. Bake for 60-75 minutes in a 325 degree oven. Prick with fork. Pour hot sauce over cake. Cool before removing from pan. Yield: 16 servings.

SAUCE

1 cup sugar
1/4 cup water

1/2 cup butter

Beat until melted. Add 2 tbsp. rum flavoring.

CHOCOLATE COOKIE SHEET CAKE

Combine in mixing bowl:

2 cups flour   2 cups sugar

Bring to boil and pour over above:

1/2 cup shortening   1 cup water
1/2 cup margarine   3 tbsp. cocoa

Add:

2 slightly beaten eggs   1 tsp. soda
1/2 cup buttermilk   2 tsp. vanilla

Mix well, pour into greased and floured 11 x 16 pan. Bake 25 minutes at 350 degrees.

ICING

1/2 cup butter   6 tbsp. milk
3 tbsp. cocoa

Bring above to boil. Add 1 box confectioners sugar and beat until smooth. Add 1 cup chopped pecans or walnuts and 2 tsp. vanilla. Spread over hot cake. Yield: 24 squares. This is excellent cut into 1-inch squares for morning coffees or afternoon teas.

SKILLET COFFEE CAKE

3/4 cup butter or
  margarine
1½ cups margarine
1½ cups sugar
2 eggs
1½ cups sifted all-purpose
  flour

1/2 tsp. salt
1 tsp. salt
1 tsp. almond flavoring
Slivered almonds
Sugar

Melt butter and add to sugar in mixing bowl. Beat
in eggs one at a time. Add flour, salt and flavoring
and mix well. Pour batter into large iron skillet
which has been lined with aluminum foil. (Leave
excess foil on either side for later use). Cover
top with slivered almonds and sprinkle with gran-
ulated sugar. Bake 30-40 minutes in a 350 degree
oven. Remove cake from the pan with the foil and
when cool, wrap tightly in the foil to store. Do
not try to peel the foil while the cake is still warm
for it will stick. This is a very rich coffee
cake. A small serving is all you can eat.

ANGEL CAKE - CHOCOLATE SAUCE

Melt 2 6-ounce pkgs. semi-sweet chocolate morsels
in double boiler with 2½ tbsp. water. Add 2 egg
yolks one at a time. Beat well. Beat 2 egg whites
until stiff and add 2 tbsp. confectioners' sugar.
Add 1 cup whipped cream and 1/2 cup chopped nuts.
Gently fold egg white mixture into chocolate mixture.
Break 1 angel cake into small pieces and put in Pyrex
dish. Pour half the sauce over and repeat layers.
Chill in refrigerator 24 hours. Cut into squares and
top with whipped cream. Yield: 12 servings.

RUM CAKE

1 pkg. yellow cake mix	1 cup salad oil
1 3 oz. pkg. instant vanilla pudding	1 cup water
	1 tsp. vanilla
4 eggs	2 tsp. rum flavoring

Combine all ingredients and beat for 10 minutes. Pour into well buttered tube pan. Bake for 45 minutes in a 350 degree oven. Keep warm and cover with warm rum sauce. Yield: 16 servings.

RUM SAUCE

1 cup sugar	1/2 cup water
1 tsp. vanilla	2 tsp. rum flavoring

Combine sugar and water, boil for 3 minutes. Add flavorings and pour over cake while warm. (This is my favorite Rum Cake recipe).

POUND CAKE

1 cup butter	3 cups all-purpose flour
1/2 cup shortening	1 tsp. vanilla
3 cups sugar	1 tsp. lemon extract
5 eggs	1/2 tsp. baking powder
1 cup milk	

Cream butter, shortening and sugar. Add eggs one at a time. Add milk alternately with flour and baking powder mixture. Stir in extracts and pour into 10 inch tube pan. Bake for 1 hour at 350 degrees and then for 15 minutes or until cake tests done at 325 degrees.

ORANGE POUND CAKE

1 pkg. yellow cake mix

4 eggs

2/3 cup salad oil

1 pkg. orange gelatin

3/4 cup orange juice
   concentrate

Combine cake mixture and beat for 5 minutes. Bake
in a tube pan for 45 minutes at 325 degrees. Turn
out on rack and while cooling make sauce:

1 cup orange juice

1 cup confectioners sugar

Cook juice and sugar until dissolved and bubbling.
(3-5 minutes). While hot spoon over cake.

FUDGE CAKE

1 cup butter

4 oz. bitter chocolate

2 cups sugar

4 eggs

1 cup flour

1 tsp. vanilla

1 cup chopped nuts

Melt butter and chocolate over low heat. Mix eggs
and sugar and add flour. Add chocolate mixture,
vanilla and nuts to flour mixture and mix. Pour in
two 8 inch square pans which have been greased and
floured. Bake for 45 to 50 minutes in a 275 degree
oven.

ICING

1/2 cup butter

2 oz. unsweetened chocolate

1 box confectioners sugar

5 tbsp. evaporated milk

1 tsp. evaporated milk

Melt butter and chocolate. Add sugar, milk and
vanilla. Mix until creamy.

STRAWBERRY ANGEL FOOD CAKE

Angel food cake
Large pkg. frozen straw-
  berries, drained
Small can crushed pine
  apple, drained

16 marshmallows, cut up
1/2 tsp. vanilla
4 cups whipped topping

Cut cake in 3 layers. Ice with strawberries and topping mixture. Keep in refrigerator after iced. Yields: 12-15 servings.

CHOCOLATE CHIP - ALMOND PIE

6 small chocolate
  bars with almonds
17 marshmallows
1/2 cup milk
1 cup heavy cream, whipped

1/2 cup chocolate chip
1/2 cup slivered almonds
1 baked graham cracker
  crust

Melt chocolate bars and marshmallows in milk in top of double boiler. Cool. Fold in whipped cream, chocolate chips and slivered almonds. Pour into graham cracker crust. Garnish with shaved chocolate. Refrigerate for at least 4 hours.

PEANUT BUTTER ICE CREAM PIE

4 tbsp. peanut butter
4 tbsp. light brown
  sugar

1 pint vanilla ice cream
Crushed peanuts
Graham cracker crust

Melt peanut butter and brown sugar in saucepan. Add ice cream and stir until mixture is well blended. Pour into graham cracker crust. Sprinkle crushed peanuts on top. Freeze.

86

GRASSHOPPER PIE AND CHOCOLATE WAFER CRUST

24 marshmallows
1/2 cup milk
1/4 cup creme de menthe

1 cup heavy cream
9 inch chocolate wafer
crust

Melt marshmallows in milk. Let cool. Add creme de menthe. Whip cream and fold into mixture.

CRUST

3/4 cup chocolate cookie crumbs
3 oz. butter, melted

Combine crumbs and butter and press into a 9 inch pan.

MILLIONAIRE PIE

2 cups confectioners
sugar
1/4 cup butter
2 eggs
1 tsp. vanilla
2 9 inch baked pie
shells
1 cup heavy cream

$2\frac{1}{2}$ tbsp. confectioners
sugar
1/2 tsp. plain gelatin
1 lb can crushed
pineapple
1/2 cup maraschino
cherries, chopped
1/4 cup chopped pecans

Cream 2 cups sugar, butter eggs and vanilla. Spread evenly in baked pie shells. Refrigerate. Whip cream, $2\frac{1}{2}$ tsp. sugar and gelatin. Fold drained pineapple, cherries and nuts into whipped cream mixture. Top pies with this mixture and refrigerate. Yield: 12-16 servings.

WILLIAMSBURG'S RUM CREAM PIE

1 envelope unflavored
  gelatin
5 egg yolks
1 cup sugar

1/3 cup dark rum
1½ cups heavy cream
Unsweetened chocolate
Crumb crust

Soften gelatin in 1/2 cup cold water. Place over
low heat and bring almost to a boil, stirring to
dissolve. Beat egg yolks and sugar until very light.
Stir gelatin into egg mixture; cool. Gradually add
rum, beating constantly. Whip cream until it stands
in soft peaks and fold into gelatin mixture. Cool,
until mixture begins to set, then spoon into crumb
crust and chill until firm enough to cut. Grate
unsweetened chocolate over top before serving.

CRUMB CRUST

2¼ cups graham cracker
  crumbs
1/2 cup melted butter

2 tbsp. sugar
1 tsp. cinnamon

Combine ingredients and press into 9 inch pie pan.
Chill.

BUTTERMILK RAISIN PIE

1 cup buttermilk
1 cup sugar
1 cup raisins
1 tbsp. butter

1/2 tsp. salt
1/2 tsp. cinnamon
1 egg, beaten
1/2 tsp. vanilla

Mix ingredients, except vanilla and bring to a boil.
Boil one minute. Let cool and add vanilla. Put
filling into an unbaked pie shell. Top with pie
crust strips and bake for 30-40 minutes in a 325
degree oven.

CORNMEAL PIE

1½ cups sugar
1½ cups brown sugar
1/2 cup butter, melted
3 eggs, separated
1½ tsp. vanilla

1/2 cup light cream
1/2 cup corn meal
1/2 cup pecans, chopped
1/2 cup coconut
1 unbaked 10 inch crust

Blend sugars and butter. Add beaten egg yolks, vanilla, cream and cornmeal. Add nuts and coconut. Add lightly beaten egg whites and blend. Bake for 35 minutes in a 350 degree oven.

COCONUT ICE BOX PIE

1 cup sugar
1 cup sweet milk
2 tbsp. flour
1 egg, slightly beaten

1 tsp. vanilla
Small package fresh
    frozen coconut
1 baked pie shell

Combine sugar, flour, sweet milk and egg and cook until thick. Add vanilla and 1/2 pkg. coconut. Pour into prebaked pie shell. Top with whipped cream and sprinkle with part of remaining coconut. Refrigerate until ready to serve.

MACAROON PIE

12 saltines, crushed
12 dates, chopped
1/2 cup chopped pecans
1 cup sugar

1/4 tsp. baking powder
3 egg whites, beaten
    stiff, but not dry
1 tsp. almond extract

Mix together crackers, dates, pecans, sugar and baking powder. Fold into egg whites and extract. Pour into a buttered pie plate. Bake for 30 minutes in a 350 degree oven.

SPRINGTIME TORTE

1 box yellow cake mix
1/3 cup water
1 cup orange juice
1 tsp. grated orange
  rind
4 egg yolks

4 egg whites
1/4 tsp. cream of tartar
1 cup sugar
2 cups heavy cream

Mix first 5 ingredients and beat with an electric
mixer for 4 minutes on medium speed. Pour into
2 9 inch cake pans which have been greased and
wax paper put into bottom. Top with meringue made
with 4 egg whites beaten stiff with 1/4 tsp. cream
of tartar and 1 cup sugar. Bake for 40 minutes in
a 350 degree oven. Cool completely before removing
from pans. Frost with 2 cups heavy cream, whipped
and sweetened to taste. Refrigerate. Serve with
sweetened fresh strawberries.

BANANA PINEAPPLE CAKE

3 cups plain flour
2 cups sugar
1 tsp. soda
1 tsp. salt
1 tsp. cinnamon
1 8 oz. can crushed
  pineapple with juice

1½ cups salad oil
3 eggs
1½ tsp. vanilla
2 cups diced bananas

Mix all ingredients together (do not use mixer).
Put in greased and floured tube pan. Bake at least
1 hour, 20 minutes in a 350 degree oven. Cool
completely before removing from pan.

SUNDAY DOWN SOUTH

At one time the Tearoom offered the Sunday Down South Buffet. It was reminiscent of a traditional Sunday meal in the Old South when families gathered at home for a huge meal after church. The buffet was sinfully laden with varied and tempting foods.

The menu changed weekly as well as seasonally to insure freshness and variety. Each Sunday meal included seven salads, freshly baked bread, home made desserts and the grand dame of the South, fried chicken. Also, the buffet boasted enticing vegetable casseroles which are rarely included in restaurant fare. These became somewhat of a special specialty. Based on the premise that simplicity is often a characteristic of delicious food, the following recipes are not complicated, just delicious.

Served amidst the sound of splashing water, lush greenery, and fresh air, courtyard dining was avilable on lazy spring, summer or fall afternoons. At times, there was a strolling musician to please old and young alike.

Sunday Down South was more than just having lunch. You could enjoy meandering to the front lawn of Carter's Court where, weather permitting, there was some type of family entertainment. Guests sat on church pews and enjoyed not only the tranquility but the lingering atmosphere of a traditional Sunday Down South. The afternoon was sure to satisfy anyone's longing to escape the chaos of the modern world and return to a more leisurely pace.

STRAWBERRY - LEMON CONGEALED SALAD

1 3 oz. pkg. strawberry
   gelatin
1 cup boiling water
1 can strawberry pie
   filling
1 3 oz. pkg. lemon
   gelatin
1 cup boiling water

1/3 cup mayonnaise
1 3 oz. pkg. cream
   cheese
1 8 3/4 oz. can crushed
   pineapple, drained
1/2 cup cup heavy cream,
   whipped

Dissolve strawberry gelatin in 1 cup boiling water;
stir in pie filling. Pour into 9 x 9 dish; chill
until partially set. Dissolve lemon gelatin in 1
cup boiling water. Beat mayonnaise and cream cheese
with mixer. Beat in lemon gelatin. Fold in pineapple and whipped cream. Spread on strawberry layer.
Chill. Cut in squares to serve.

CONGEALED SPICED PEACH SALAD

1 16 oz. can sliced
   peaches
1/4 cup vinegar
1/2 cup sugar
12 whole cloves

1/8 tsp. cinnamon
1 3 oz. pkg. orange
   gelatin
3/4 cup cold water

Drain peaches, saving 1 cup syrup. Chop peaches
coarsely. Bring syrup, vinegar, sugar and spices
to a boil and simmer for 10 minutes. Strain syrup
and discard cloves. Dissolve gelatin in hot syrup.
Add cold water and peaches. Chill until slightly
thickened. Pour into mold or 9 x 9 dish.

CHRISTMAS RIBBON SALAD

1 6 oz. pkg. lime gelatin
1 6 oz. pkg. raspberry
  gelatin
1 3 oz. pkg. lemon
  gelatin
5 cups boiling water
1 cup miniature marsh-
  mallows

3 cups cold water
6 oz. cream cheese,
  softened
1/2 cup mayonnaise
1 cup heavy cream,
  whipped
1 20½ oz. can crushed
  pineapple, drained

Dissolve gelatin flavors separately, using 2 cups
boiling water each for lime and raspberry gelatins;
1 cup boiling water for lemon gelatin. Stir marshmallows into lemon gelatin; set aside. Add 1½ cups
cold water to lime gelatin and pour into 9 x 13
dish. Chill until set, but not firm. Meanwhile, add
1½ cups cold water to raspberry gelatin and set
aside at room temperature. Add cream cheese to
lemon mixture; beat until blended. Chill until
slightly thickened. Then blend in mayonnaise, whipped cream, and crushed pineapple. Chill until thick;
spoon gently (do not pour) over lime layer. Chill
until set. Meanwhile, chill raspberry gelatin until
thickened. Spoon gently over lemon layer. Chill until firm. Cut into squares and serve on lettuce
leaf. (12 servings)

LIME FLUFF

1 16 oz. carton cottage
  cheese
1 3 oz. pkg. lime
  gelatin

1 14 oz. can crushed
  pineapple, drained
1 6 oz. carton whipped
  topping

Sprinkle gelatin over cottage cheese in a large
bowl. Mix. Add pineapple and whipped topping. Mix
thoroughly. Chill until served.

MARINATED GREEN VEGETABLES

1 16 oz. can small peas
1 16 oz. can cut green
  beans
1 can Chinese vegetables
1 cup chopped green
  pepper

1/2 cup chopped onion
1 4 oz. can chopped
  pimentos
1 cup white vinegar
1 cup sugar
1 cup vegetable oil

Drain canned vegetables. Mix vegetables gently.
Make marinade of vinegar, sugar and oil. Pour over
vegetables. Refrigerate for 24 hours before serving.

SAUERKRAUT SALAD

2 lbs sauerkraut
1 cup sugar
1 finely chopped large
  onion
1 finely chopped green
  pepper

1 cup finely chopped
  celery
1 2 oz. jar pimento,
  chopped
1/2 cup vegetable oil
1/4 cup wine vinegar

Drain sauerkraut; add sugar. Let sugar and sauerkraut stand for 10 minutes. Drain off any liquid.
Combine chopped vegetables in bowl. Mix oil and
vinegar. Pour over vegetables. Add sauerkraut and
toss. Refrigerate for 24 hours before serving.

TUNA MOUSSE

2 envelopes gelatin
  softened in 1/2 cup
  cold water
1 cup mayonnaise
2 tbsp. lemon juice
1 cup chopped celery
1/2 cup chopped stuffed
    olives
2 tbsp. chopped chives

4 hard boiled eggs,
  mashed
2 7 oz. cans white tuna,
  drained and mashed
2 tsp. horseradish,
  drained
1/2 tsp. salt
1/4 tsp. hot sauce
1 cup heavy cream,
  whipped

Heat softened gelatin until dissolved. Add mayonnaise and lemon juice. Mix with a wire whisk. Add remaining ingredients except the cream. Mix thoroughly. Chill for about 1 hour. Fold in whipped cream. Pour into 9 x 9 square dish. Cut into squares to serve.

VEGETABLES

BROCCOLI - RICE CASSEROLE

2 cups cooked rice
8 oz. American processed
cheese, cubed
2 10 oz. pkg. broccoli
cuts, cooked and
drained
1 can cream of chicken
soup

1 can water chestnuts,
drained and sliced

1/2 cup milk
1 tsp. Worcestershire
sauce
Salt and pepper to taste
Bread crumbs

Combine hot rice and broccoli with cheese. Allow
cheese to melt before adding other ingredients.
Place in buttered casserole. Sprinkle bread crumbs
on top. Bake for 20 to 30 minutes in a 350 degree
oven.

ASPARAGUS AND ENGLISH PEA CASSEROLE

1 16 oz. can peas
1 16 oz. can asparagus
cuts
1 8 oz. can mushroom
pieces

1 can mushroom soup
1/2 cup cracker crumbs
1/2 cup grated Cheddar
cheese

Drain vegetables and mushroom pieces. Place half
amount of the ingredients above in order listed
in a buttered casserole. Repeat layers. Bake for
30 minutes in a 350 degree oven.

SPINACH AND TOMATO BAKE

4 medium tomatoes
1 10 oz. pkg. frozen
  chopped spinach, thawed
  and well drained
1/2 cup herb stuffing mix

1 tbsp. chopped onion
1 egg, beaten
1/4 cup butter, melted
1/4 cup Parmesan cheese

Slice each tomato into 2 thick slices. Let drain
if they should be watery. Place in a greased baking
dish in a single layer, sliced side facing up.
Place remaining ingredients in a bowl and mix well.
Make mounds of the spinach mixture on each tomato
slice. Bake for 15 minutes a 350 degree oven.

RICE SUPREME

1 cup long grain rice
1/2 cup butter or
  margarine
2 cups chopped celery
1 cup chopped onion

1 can beef consomme
1 can cream of mushroom
  soup
1/2 tsp. curry powder

In large skillet brown rice in butter, stirring
often over medium heat. Add celery and onion and
continue cooking for 5 minutes. Remove from heat;
add consomme, soup, and curry powder. Mix well with
a whisk. Pour mixture into a greased 1½ quart baking dish. Cover and bake for 1 hour in a 350 degree
oven.

ORIENTAL VEGETABLE CASSEROLE

1 16 oz. can French
  style green beans
1 16 oz. can Chinese
  vegetables
2 cans cream of mushroom
  soup

1 lb. Cheddar cheese,
  grated
2 3 oz. cans Chinese
  noodles

Drain the vegetables. Layer half of all the ingredients in a greased casserole in the order given. Make second layer in the same order. Bake for 30 minutes in a 350 degree oven.

EASY SPINACH CASSEROLE

3 10 oz. pkg. frozen
  chopped spinach, thawed
  and well drained

1 pkg. onion soup mix
1/2 cup butter, melted
1/2 tsp. nutmeg

Mix ingredients. Bake in a buttered casserole for 30 minutes in a 350 degree oven.

SWEET POTATO PUDDING

4 cups grated or
  shredded raw sweet
  potatoes
2 cups sugar
1 1/3 cups milk

4 eggs, beaten
1/2 heaping tsp.
  allspice
1/2 heaping tsp.
  cinnamon

Peel and grate sweet potatoes. Mix with other ingredients. Bake in a shallow greased dish for 1 hour in a 350 degree oven.

CORN PUDDING

2½ cups cream style
   corn
5 tbsp. flour
1 tbsp. sugar

1 tsp. salt
1/4 cup butter, melted
3/4 cup milk
3 eggs, beaten

Mix corn and flour with a wire whisk. Add other
ingredients and mix. Bake in a buttered dish for
1 hour in a 325 degree oven. (6 servings)

EGGPLANT CASSEROLE

2 large eggplants
2 cups canned spaghetti
   sauce
3 medium onions, sliced

1 cup Mozzarella
   cheese
1/4 cup grated Parmesan
   cheese

Peel and slice eggplant into 1/2 inch slices. Boil
in small amount of water for 10 minutes. Layer eggplant, onion, sauce and Mozzarella in a greased
casserole. Repeat layers. Top with Parmesan. Bake
for 45 minutes in a 350 degree oven. Zucchini may
be substituted for the eggplant. Do not peel but
slice and boil it the same way.

CARROT - RAISIN CASSEROLE

1/3 cup soft butter
1/2 cup sugar
3 eggs, beaten
3 cups cooked, mashed
  carrots

3/4 cup raisins
3/4 cup milk
3/4 tsp. baking powder
Grated rind of 1 lemon

Cream butter and sugar. Add eggs and mix. Blend in remaining ingredients. Bake in a buttered casserole for 30 minutes in a 350 degree oven.

QUICK AND EASY PEAS

2 1 lb. cans small
  English peas
1/4 cup butter

1/4 cup finely chopped
  onions
1 can mushroom soup

Drain peas. Saute onion in butter. Add remaining ingredients; heat and serve. You may put this in a buttered casserole, top with grated Cheddar cheese and bake for 20 minutes in a 350 degree oven.

SQUASH CASSEROLE

3 lbs. squash, yellow
  or zucchini
1 chopped onion
1/4 cup butter
3 eggs, beaten

1 can cream of mushroom
  soup
1 tsp. salt
3/4 tsp. pepper
Cracker crumbs

Cook squash and onion until tender. Drain well. Add butter and mix well. Fold in remaining ingredients. Place in a buttered casserole and top with a thin layer of cracker crumbs. Bake for 30 minutes in a 350 degree oven.

SWEET AND SOUR CHICKEN

3-4 lb. fryer or 8 split breasts
1 8 oz. bottle Russian, Casino, or Catalina dressing

2 envelopes onion soup mix
1 8 oz. jar apricot or peach jam

Place chicken in shallow greased baking pan or dish skin side up. In separate bowl, mix other ingredients and spread over chicken. Bake covered 1 hour; then uncovered 1 hour in a 300 degree oven.

HAM LOAF

2½ lbs. ground smoked ham
1/2 lb. ground fresh pork
3 eggs, beaten
1 cup bread crumbs

1 cup milk
1/4 tsp. pepper
1½ tbsp. prepared mustard
1/2 cup brown sugar
3/4 cup pineapple juice

Have your butcher grind the smoked ham and pork. Mix meat, eggs, bread crumbs, milk and pepper thoroughly. Place in a shallow baking dish. Mix mustard and brown sugar. Spread on ham loaf. Bake for 1½ hours in a 350 degree oven, basting several times with the pineapple juice.

BUFFET STROGANOFF

2 lbs. boneless sirloin,
    cut into 1 inch strips
1½ cups mushroom pieces
1/2 cup green peppers,
    sliced
1/2 cup onions, sliced

1/2 cup butter
2 cups beef stock
1/4 cup flour
1½ cups sour cream
1 tsp. salt
1/2 tsp. pepper

Saute beef in butter until brown. Add mushrooms, peppers, and onions. Saute. Add beef stock (if beef stock is made from cubes, reduce salt to ½ tsp.) Simmer 15 minutes. Mix flour with sour cream. Add to beef mixture, stirring well to thicken. Simmer an additional 15 minutes. Serve over hot buttered noodles.

CHICKEN CASSEROLE

1½ cups chopped green
    onions
2 cups chopped celery
2 tbsp. butter
1 pkg. herb stuffing mix
1/2 cup butter
1 cup water
3 cups cooked, chopped
    chicken

1/2 cup mayonnaise
3/4 tsp. salt
1/4 tsp. pepper
2 eggs, beaten
1¼ cups milk
1 can cream of mushroom
    soup

Saute onion and celery in 2 tbsp. butter. Meanwhile spread half herb stuffing mix in a greased 9 x 13 baking dish. Heat ½ cup butter and the water and pour over mix. In a large bowl, mix chicken, sauteed onion and celery, mayonnaise, salt and pepper. Spread over crumb mixture in baking dish. Cover and refrigerate over night. Remove from refrigerator one hour before baking. Spread soup over casserole and sprinkle remaining herb stuffing mix on top. Bake for 1 hour in a 350 degree oven.

EASY JAMBALAYA

1 large onion, chopped
1 green pepper, chopped
1/2 cup butter
2 cups chopped cooked
. ham
3 cups cooked shrimp

1/2 tsp. salt
1/4 tsp. pepper
1 8 oz. can tomato sauce
1 8 oz. can tomato puree
1/2 cup dry sherry
2 cups cooked rice

Saute onion and pepper in butter. In large mixing
bowl blend all ingredients. Bake in a greased 3
quart casserole for 40 minutes in a 350 degree oven.

BUFFET MEAT LOAF

1½ lbs. ground beef
1 cup herb stuffing mix
1 8 oz. can tomato sauce
1 egg, beaten

1½ tsp. salt
1/2 tsp. pepper
1/2 cup chopped onion
Catsup and parsley
    flakes

Mix ingredients. Shape in baking dish. Bake for 1
hour in a 350 degree oven. Before cutting into
slices, spread top of meat loaf with catsup and
sprinkle parsley flakes over catsup.

SWEET AND SOUR MEATBALLS

1½ lbs. ground round   1/2 tsp. salt
  steak   1/4 tsp. pepper
3/4 cup bread crumbs   1 8 oz. can tomato sauce
1 egg, beaten   3/4 cup catsup
1 small onion, chopped   1/2 cup sugar

Combine beef, bread crumbs, egg onion, salt and
pepper. Mix well. Shape into 1 inch balls and place
in a single or double layer in baking pan. Set aside.
In another bowl combine tomato sauce, catsup and
sugar. Pour over meatballs. Bake for 1½ hours in
a 350 degree oven. Serve over noodles or in a
chafing dish as an appetizer. This so easy because you do not have to fry all those meatballs.

TURKEY TETRAZZINI

1 cup chopped onion   3 cups chopped, cooked
1/2 cup chopped green   turkey
  pepper   1 2 oz. jar chopped
1½ cups chopped celery   pimentos
1/2 cup butter   1 8 oz. can mushroom
1 can mushroom soup   pieces
1 cup grated Cheddar   1 cup slivered almonds
  cheese   1 lb. spaghetti, cooked
1 tbsp. flour   and drained
3 cups chicken or turkey   Salt and pepper to taste
  broth

Saute onion, pepper, celery in butter. Keep over
heat and add soup, cheese and flour. Stir with a
wire whisk until it boils. Add broth. Blend. Remove from heat. Add remaining ingredients. Bake in
a greased casserole for 30 minutes in a 350 degree
oven.

WILD RICE AND OYSTER CASSEROLE

3 pints standard oysters
  drain, save liquid
5 cups beef stock
2 6 oz. pkg. long grain
  and wild rice with
  seasonings

1/2 cup butter
3 cups mushroom sauce
  (see recipe below)

Cook rice according to directions using beef stock
in place of the water. When rice is cooked, add
butter. Heat oysters in pan just long enough for
the edges to curl. Spoon half the rice mixture into
a buttered casserole. Arrange half the oysters on
top. Cover with remaining rice mixture and oysters.
Spoon mushroom sauce over all. Bake for 30 minutes
in a 325 degree oven.

Mushroom sauce for casserole:

3 tbsp. butter
1/4 cup chopped onion
3 tbsp. flour
1 cup oyster liquid

8 oz. mushroom pieces
2 tsp. curry powder
1/2 cup heavy cream

Saute onions in butter. Add flour. When bubbly, add
oyster liquid, stirring with wire whisk until thickened. Add remaining ingredients.

CAROLYN'S CHICKEN

6 strips uncooked bacon
1 cup rice
8 chicken pieces
garlic salt and pepper

1 can cream of chicken
  soup
1 can water
oregano

Line casserole with bacon strips. Add 1 cup rice
Salt and pepper chicken and place on rice. Mix
soup with water. Pour over chicken. Sprinkle
lightly with oregano. Cover with foil. Bake
1½ hours at 350 degrees.

BAKED FISH WITH SHRIMP – PARMESAN SAUCE

3 tbsp. butter
2 tbsp. flour
1/2 tsp. salt
1 cup milk
2 lbs. white fish fillets
  (ocean perch, flounder,
   sole, etc.)

1/2 lb. small cooked
  shrimp
1/4 cup Parmesan cheese,
  optional

Make a medium white sauce: melt butter in skillet,
add flour and cook until bubbly, add salt and milk,
stirring constantly. Remove from heat. Layer fish
in a buttered flat baking dish. Spread shrimp and
white sauce over fish. Sprinkle with Parmesan
cheese. Bake for 20–25 minutes in a 325 degree
oven.

WILLIAMSBURG'S SALLY LUNN BREAD

1 cup milk
1/2 cup vegetable
  shortening
1/4 cup water
4 cups sifted flour

1/3 cup sugar
2 tsp. salt
2 pkg. dry yeast
3 eggs

Heat milk, shortening, and water until warm - 120 degrees. Place milk mixture in large mixer bowl and add 1 1/3 cups of the flour, the sugar, salt and yeast. Beat on medium speed for 2 minutes. Gradually add 2/3 cup of the remaining flour and the eggs. Beat at high speed for 2 minutes. Add remaining flour and beat by hand until blended. Cover. Let rise until double - about 1½ hours. Punch dough down. Put in a well greased tube pan. Cover. Let rise about 30 minutes. Bake 40 - 50 minutes in a 350 degree oven. Remove from pan in 10 minutes.

JALAPENO CORN BREAD

1 cup yellow corn meal	1 tsp. baking soda
1 cup cream style corn	1/2 tsp. salt
1 cup grated Cheddar	2 eggs, beaten
cheese	2 Jalapeno peppers,
1/2 cup vegetable oil	chopped fine
1/2 cup buttermilk	2 tbsp. bacon drippings

Mix all ingredients in bowl except for the bacon drippings. Put bacon drippings in a 9 x 9 pan or a black skillet. Heat in oven until drippings cover bottom of pan. Pour batter into pan and bake for 20 to 25 minutes in a 400 degree oven.

PUMPKIN MUFFINS

3/4 cup brown sugar	1 3/4 cups flour
1/4 cup molasses	1 tsp. soda
1/2 cup soft butter	1/4 tsp. salt
1 egg, beaten	1/2 cup pecans, dates or
1 cup pumpkin, cooked	or raisins, chopped
and mashed	

Cream sugar, molasses and butter. Add egg and pumpkin. Blend well. Sift dry ingredients. Add to batter, beating well. Fold in pecans, dates or raisins. Bake for 20 minutes in a 350 degree oven. Makes 16 muffins.

DESSERTS

CHEESECAKE SQUARES

1/4 cup butter, melted
1 cup graham cracker
    crumbs
1 3 oz. pkg. lemon
    gelatin
1 cup boiling water

1 8 oz. pkg. cream cheese,
    softened
1 cup sugar
1 14½ oz. can evaporated
    milk, well chilled

Mix butter and crumbs. Pat in 9 x 9 square pan.
Bake crust for 8 minutes in a 375 degree oven. Set
aside. Dissolve gelatin in boiling water. Chill
until it begins to harden. Mix cream cheese and
sugar until creamy. Whip evaporated milk until it
has the consistency of whipped cream. Mix gelatin,
cream cheese mixture and whipped milk together until
it is well blended and creamy. Pour into crumb crust.
Refrigerate for at least one hour before serving.

CHOCOLATE CHESS PIE

1½ cups sugar
2 eggs, slightly beaten
1/3 cup cocoa
1/4 cup butter

1/2 cup evaporated milk
1/2 cup coconut
1/2 cup pecan pieces
1 9 inch pie shell

Mix all ingredients by hand and pour in pie shell.
Bake for 30 minutes in a 400 degree oven. Cool and
serve with vanilla ice cream or whipped cream.

ITALIAN CREAM CAKE

1/2 cup butter	1 tsp. baking soda
1/2 cup vegetable oil	2 cups flour, sifted
2 cups sugar	1 tsp. vanilla
5 eggs, separated	1 cup coconut
1 cup buttermilk	1/2 cup chopped nuts

Cream butter, oil and sugar. Add egg yolks one at
a time, beating after each addition. Stir baking
soda into buttermilk. Add small amount of flour to
batter, beating on medium speed, alternating with
buttermilk mixture. Add vanilla, coconut and pecans.
Beat egg whites in separate bowl until stiff and
fold into cake batter. Pour into a greased and
floured 9 x 13 cake pan or three 8 inch layer pans.
Bake for 45 minutes in a 325 degree oven. Cool and
ice.

ICING FOR ITALIAN CREAM CAKE

8 oz. cream cheese, softened	1 tsp. vanilla
	1/2 cup chopped nuts
1/2 cup butter, softened	
1 lb. box confectioners sugar	

Beat cream cheese and butter. Add sugar and vanilla.
Mix well. Add nuts. Beat to mix. Spread on cake.

FRENCH COCONUT PIE

3 eggs, slightly beaten	1/2 cup melted butter
1½ cups sugar	1 cup coconut
1 tsp. vanilla	1 9 inch pie shell

Add all ingredients and mix by hand. Pour into pie shell. Bake for 15 minutes in a 400 degree oven, reduce heat and continue baking 20 to 45 minutes in a 350 degree oven.

JAPANESE FRUIT PIE

Follow directions for French Coconut Pie above except add a 1 cup mixture of raisins, pecans, and coconut in place of the 1 cup of coconut.

BOURBON AND CHOCOLATE PECAN PIE

1 cup sugar	2 tbsp. bourbon
1/4 cup butter, melted	1 tsp. vanilla
3 eggs, slightly beaten	1/2 cup chopped pecans
3/4 cup light corn syrup	1/2 cup chocolate chips
1/4 tsp. salt	1 9 inch pie shell

Cream sugar and butter. Add eggs, syrup, salt, bourbon and vanilla. Mix until blended. Spread pecans and chocolate chips in bottom of pie shell. Pour filling into shell. Bake for 40 to 50 minutes in a 375 degree oven.

LEMON ICEBOX PIE

1 prepared graham
  cracker crust
1 6 oz. carton whipped
  topping

1 6 oz. can frozen
  lemonade concentrate,
  thawed
1 14 oz. can condensed milk

Beat topping, lemonade concentrate and condensed
milk in large bowl of electric mixer. Pour into pie
shell and chill an hour before serving. Frozen lime-
ade concentrate may be used in place of lemonade for
a lime pie.

SMOOTH DESSERT OR PIE FILLING

5 cups boiling water
1 6 oz. pkg. gelatin
  (strawberry, raspberry,
  peach, blueberry, etc.)

1 pkg. vanilla pudding
  (not instant type)
1 6 oz. carton whipped
  topping

Dissolve gelatin and pudding in boiling water.
Chill until it just begins to congeal - it will
be shaky. In large bowl of electric mixer beat
gelatin mixture and whipped topping. Return to
refrigerator until serving time.

113

PISTACHIO NUT CAKE

1 white cake mix	2/3 cup vegetable oil
1 box instant pistachio	1 cup club soda
pudding	1 cup chopped nuts
4 eggs	(English walnuts or pecans)

Put all ingredients in large bowl of electric mixer and blend well. Pour into greased and floured 9 x 13 or three layer pans. Bake for 40 minutes in a 350 degree oven. Cool. Frost with Pistachio Frosting. Refrigerate this cake when frosted.

PISTACHIO FROSTING

1 9 oz. carton whipped	1 cup milk
topping	
1 box instant pistachio	
pudding	

Mix frosting ingredients in large bowl of electric mixer. Let stand 10 minutes before spreading on cake.

FEATHERY FUDGE CAKE

2/3 cup soft butter
1 3/4. cups sugar
2 eggs
1 tsp. vanilla
2½ squares baking
  chocolate, melted
  and cooled

2½ cups sifted cake
  flour
1¼ tsp. baking soda
1/2 tsp. salt
1¼ cups ice water

Cream butter, sugar, eggs and vanilla until very
fluffy and light in color - about 5 minutes on high
speed of mixer. Blend in chocolate. Sift flour, soda
and salt together. Add flour mixture to batter alternately with ice water, beating after each addition.
Bake in greased and floured 9 x 13 or 2 layer pans
for 25 to 30 minutes in a 350 degree oven. Cool and
frost with Chocolate Satin Frosting.

CHOCOLATE SATIN FROSTING

3½ squares baking
  chocolate, melted
3 cups confectioners
  sugar

4½ tbsp. hot water
1 egg
1/2 cup butter
1½ tsp. vanilla

Blend sugar and hot water in electric mixer. Add
other ingredients. Mix well.

PEANUT BUTTER CAKE

1/2 cup butter
1½ cups sugar
2 egg yolks, beaten
  well
1/2 cup buttermilk
1 tsp. baking soda
1/2 cup water

2 heaping tbsp. peanut
  butter
1½ cups sifted cake
  flour
1 tsp. baking powder
2 egg whites, stiffly
  beaten

Cream butter and sugar. Add egg yolks. Mix buttermilk with baking soda; add water to buttermilk mixture. Mix peanut butter with butter, sugar and egg yolks. Sift cake flour and baking powder together. Add flour mixture and buttermilk mixture alternately to batter, beating well after each addition. Fold egg whites into batter. Bake in a greased and floured 9 x 13 or 2 round or square pans for 25 to 30 minutes in a 375 degree oven. Cool and frost with peanut butter frosting.

PEANUT BUTTER FROSTING

1 lb. box confectioners
  sugar
4 tbsp. vegetable
  shortening
4 heaping tbsp. peanut
  butter

1/2 to 3/4 cup heavy
  cream
1 tsp. vanilla

Mix all ingredients well - adding 1/2 cup heavy cream in beginning. Add more if needed until spreading consistency is reached.

SPECIAL DAYS AT THE RESTAURANT

If you hear the sound of much gaiety and laughter, it may be a "Special Day" at Miss Daisy's. The honoree may be a national celebrity or a new bride, or a "Special Day" may benefit a charity. It may be a time for reverie and reflection, or fun and frolic. It may be a time to look forward to and a time to look back upon. A special event is any event when food and other than the regular menu is served.

Most homes today were not designed to accommodate large numbers of people. Accordingly, since the restaurant was once a home, it becomes the ideal place to entertain a large group and still maintain the warmth of an "at home" atmosphere. With masses of fresh flowers or greenery and a delectable menu, the stage is set for a wedding reception, a press reception or whatever your imagination allows.

One year the restaurant offered a Merry Month of May teatime. In mid-afternoon it became a haven for tired shoppers. Many varieties of tea were offered with crumpets. However, the specialty of the house, as always, was hospitality - Southern style.

If the guests cannot stay for lunch, the lunch can go with the guests. For lack of time, many tour groups prefer to have lunch while en route to the next attraction.

Whether you prefer simple food or foods with a flair, sunlight or candlelight - whether you plan to entertain the President of the United States, or your mother-in-law, Miss Daisy can make it a special event catered to your whims.

MISS DAISY'S BOX LUNCH

Fried Chicken   Ham Salad in Pastry Cups

Pimento Cheese Sandwich

Fresh Fruit   Chess Tarts

Iced Tea

FRIED CHICKEN

8 pieces chicken,	1/2 tsp. salt
unskinned	1/2 tsp. pepper
2 cups vegetable oil	1 tsp. paprika
2 eggs	2 cups flour
1 cup buttermilk	

Beat eggs and milk with fork and add salt, pepper and paprika. Dip chicken into egg mixture. Dip into flour. Fry in hot oil. Brown on one side, turn and brown on other. Cover pan and cook on low heat for 20 minutes.

PIMENTO CHEESE SANDWICH

See Index for page number of recipe.

HAM SALAD

2 cups cubed cooked ham   1/2 cup mayonnaise
1 cup diced celery   1/4 cup light cream
1/2 cup diced apples

Combine ingredients and serve in lettuce cup or pastry shells.

CHESS TARTS

3 eggs, beaten   6 tbsp. buttermilk
1½ cups sugar   1/2 cup melted butter
1 tsp. vanilla   6-8 tart shells

Mix ingredients. Pour into tart shells and bake for 30 minutes in a 350 degree oven, then 10 more minutes in a 300 degree oven until tarts are set.

UNITED STATES SENATOR'S RECEPTION

Ham and Rolls   Shrimp Cucumber Rounds

Bowls of Fresh Fruit with
Sour Cream or Confectioners Sugar

Platter of Assorted Cheeses

Pecan Sandies   Fudge Cake Squares

Orange Frost

SHRIMP CUCUMBER ROUNDS

5 dozen rounds of whole   5 dozen slices cucumber
  wheat bread   5 dozen small shrimp,
1¼ cups cream cheese,   cooked
  whipped

Cut 20 slices of whole wheat bread into rounds,
using three rounds per slice. Spread each round
with 1 tsp. whipped cream cheese. Top with slice
of cucumber and a small cooked shrimp. (You may
want to add a small amount of cream cheese to the
top of the cucumber slice to secure the shrimp.)

PECAN SANDIES

2 cups butter	2 tbsp. water
1/4 cup confectioners	4 cups sifted flour
sugar	2 cups chopped pecans
4 tsp. vanilla extract	Confectioners sugar

Cream butter and sugar. Add vanilla and stir in water and flour. Blend well. Fold in pecans. Form into small (1½ inch) crescents. Place on ungreased baking sheet and bake for 20 minutes in a 300 degree oven. Remove from oven and dust with confectioners sugar while hot,

FUDGE CAKE SQUARES

See Index for page number of recipe.

ORANGE FROST

3 12 oz. cans frozen orange juice, diluted
8 quarts ginger ale, chilled
2 quarts orange sherbert

Combine orange juice and ginger ale and pour over ornage. sherbert. Float slices of orange and sprigs of mint in punch bowl for garnishes. Yield 100 4 oz. servings.

AFTERNOON TEA

Raisin Biscuits   Tea Cakes

Crumpets   Lemon Curd

Assorted Teas

RAISIN BISCUITS

2½ cups flour   4 tsp. baking powder
1/3 cup shortening   1 tsp. salt
3/4 cup milk   1 tbsp. sugar
1 egg   1 cup seedless raisins

Sift sugar, salt and baking powder with flour. Break egg in small bowl and mix well, add milk and raisins. Mix into dough with milk, egg and raisins, using spoon. Turn onto a well floured board and knead until smooth. Roll out to 1/2 inch thick, cut with tea biscuit cutter. Bake for 10-12 minutes in a 400 degree oven.

TEA CAKES

2 cups sugar	1/2 tsp. soda
1/2 cup butter	2 tsp. baking powder
1/2 cup shortening	1 tsp. vanilla
1/2 cup buttermilk	Flour sufficient to
3 eggs	make a soft dough

Cream butter and shortening, add sugar, then beaten eggs. Into one cup flour sift soda and baking powder. Add this to the sugar mixture. Add milk and vanilla and enough flour to make a soft dough. Turn onto a floured board, knead until smooth. Roll out 1/4 inch thick. Cut in any shape. Bake about 10 minutes in a 350 degree oven or until brown. Yield: 6 dozen.

CRUMPETS

4 cups flour	2 eggs
1 cup milk warmed	1 tsp. salt
until tepid	
1 compressed yeast cake dissolved in	
1/2 cup water	

Beat eggs together well. Add milk, yeast and flour, making a stiff batter. Let rise until light, covering bowl to prevent crusting over top. When risen, have a griddle hot and greased. Pour on a large spoonful carefully as large as batter cakes. Bake rather slowly turning when one side is browned. Butter and serve with Lemon Curd.

LEMON CURD

5 egg yolks   1 cup sugar
1 egg white   3 tbsp. butter
1/4 cup lemon juice

Mix together well, cook in double boiler until
thick and clear, stirring constantly. Store in
jar and keep refrigerated. Serve with crumpets,
teacakes, gingerbread or use as a filling.

NOTES

REMEMBER – Each recipe serves 6 – 8 people unless
         otherwise noted.

Shrimp Mold, Assorted Crackers, Tomato Juice

Baked Chicken Piquant with Rice

Green Beans with Water Chestnuts

Stuffed Squash

Rolls and Butter

Fruited Rum Ice Cream and Wedding Cookies

Coffee or Iced Tea

SHRIMP MOLD

1 can tomato soup
1 8 oz. pkg. cream cheese
2 envelopes plain
  gelatin, softened for
  5 minutes in 1/2 cup
  cold water
2 lbs. cooked small shrimp
1/4 cup diced green
  onion

1/4 cup diced green
  pepper
1 cup diced celery
1/4 tsp. each: salt,
  pepper, celery salt,
  onion salt, hot sauce
1 cup mayonnaise
2 tbsp. drained horse-
  radish

Heat soup and cream cheese. Stir with wire whisk
until cheese is melted. Some small lumps will remain.
Add dissolved gelatin to hot soup and cheese mixture.
Remove from heat and stir well. Add remaining in-
gedients. Pour into a well greased 1 quart ring
mold. Refrigerate until set. Garnish as desired.
Yield: 40-50 servings as an appetizer spread.

BAKED CHICKEN PIQUANT WITH RICE

3 cups Burgundy wine   1 tsp. ginger
1 cup soy sauce   1 tsp. oregano
1 cup salad oil   1/4 cup brown sugar
1 cup water   8 chicken breast halves
4 cloves minced garlic   1 lb. box long grain rice

Combine all ingredients except chicken and rice.
Spread rice in bottom of 9 x 13 baking dish. Place
chicken breasts on top of rice. Pour Burgundy mixture over all. Cover with foil and bake for 1½ hours
in a 350 degree oven. Add more water if rice becomes
dry during last half hour of baking.

GREEN BEANS AND WATER CHESTNUTS

3 16 oz. cans green   1/4 tsp. each; pepper,
  beans, whole or cut   onion salt
2 cans cream of mush-   1 can French fried onion
  room soup   rings, crushed
2 cans water chestnuts,
  drained and sliced

Mix all ingredients except onion rings. Put in a
buttered 2 quart casserole. Sprinkle crushed onion
rings on top. Bake for 30 minutes in a 350 degree
oven.

STUFFED SQUASH

5 medium yellow squash	1/2 tsp. salt
1/2 cup minced onion	1/4 tsp. pepper
1/4 cup butter	1 cup grated cheddar
1/4 cup bread crumbs	cheese
1/4 cup minced celery	Paprika

Boil whole squash in salted water just until tender. Cool, split lengthwise and scoop out pulp. Saute onion and celery in butter. Add remaining ingredients and squash pulp. Stuff shells with this mixture, top with grated cheese and paprika. Bake for 20-30 minutes in a 350 degree oven.

FRUITED RUM ICE CREAM

1/2 gallon vanilla ice cream
1 cup mixture of diced candied cherries, candied
  pineapple, chopped black walnuts or pecans
1/4 to 1/2 cup dark rum

Soften ice cream in large bowl. Mix in the candied fruit and rum. Return to freezer until serving time.

WEDDING COOKIES

1 cup soft butter	2¼ cups flour
1/2 cup sifted con- fectioners sugar	1/4 tsp. salt
	3/4 cup finely chopped
1 tsp. vanilla	pecans

Mix butter, sugar and vanilla thoroughly. Blend
flour and salt; stir into butter mixture. Mix
in pecans. Roll into 1 inch balls. Place on ungreased baking sheet. Bake 10 to 12 minutes in
a 400 degree oven. While still warm, roll in sifted
confectioners sugar. Cool. Roll in sugar again.

Marinated Artichoke Hearts, Shrimp and Mushrooms

Cherry Tomatoes Filled with Chicken Salad

Sliced Smoked Turkey, Roast Beef, Ham Cheese,
Breads and Spreads for Sandwiches

Asparagus Sandwiches

Hot Sausage Cheese Balls   Seafood Casserole

Cream Cheese Roquefort Mold with Assorted
Fresh fruit cuts and Crackers

Wedding Cake

Coffee   Punch   Champagne

MARINATED ARTICHOKE HEARTS, SHRIMP AND MUSHROOMS

2 14 oz. cans tiny arti-   2 pkgs. Italian dressing
choke hearts, drained   mix
2 lb. cooked shrimp
2 4 oz. cans whole button
mushrooms, drained

Put artichoke hearts, shrimp and mushrooms in bowl.
Mix dressing according to package directions. Pour
dressing over all and marinate for 8 hours.

ASPARAGUS SANDWICHES

1 loaf bread, light, whole grain variety	1 can asparagus spears, drained
1/2 cup softened butter	1/4 cup melted butter
1 cup Parmesan cheese	Paprika

Cut crusts from bread slices. Spread each slice
with softened butter and sprinkle with Parmesan
cheese. Roll each asparagus spear diagonally in
a piece of bread. Secure with toothpicks. Before
baking brush each roll with melted butter and
sprinkle with remaining Parmesan cheese and some
paprika. Bake 10-12 minutes in a 400 degree oven.

SAUSAGE CHEESE BALLS

1 lb. sausage, hot or mild	3 cups biscuit mix
1 lb. extra sharp Cheddar cheese, grated	

Mix ingredients well. Drop by tsp. on ungreased
baking sheet. Bake for 15-20 minutes in a 350
degree oven. Serve hot.

SEAFOOD CASSEROLE

1/2 lb. mushrooms, chopped
1/2 butter
1 cup cooked diced lobster
1 cup crab meat
2 cups cooked shrimp
1/4 cup butter

1/4 cup flour
1/2 tsp. salt
1/4 tsp. pepper
2 cups milk
2 tbsp. sherry
1 cup grated American cheese

Saute mushrooms in 1/2 cup butter. Add seafood.
Make a medium white sauce: melt 1/4 cup butter,
add flour and cook until bubbly. Add salt and
pepper, remove from heat. Add milk, bring to
boil, stirring constantly. Add white sauce and
sherry to seafood mixture. Mix well. Pour into
a greased 9 x 13 baking dish. Top with cheese.
Bake 20-30 minutes in a 350 degree oven.

CREAM CHEESE AND ROQUEFORT MOLD

2 envelopes plain gelatin softened for 5 minutes in 1/2 cup cold water
1 8 oz. pkg. cream cheese, softened
1 1½ oz. pkg. roquefort cheese

1/2 tsp. salt
1 cup heavy cream, whipped
1 cup chopped walnuts, optional

Heat softened gelatin until dissolved. Mix the
cheeses together in electric mixer. Add gelatin,
salt and whipped cream. Beat until blended. Pour
into 1 quart mold (greased). Chill until set.
Unmold, garnish with watercress, mint or parsley
and serve with fresh fruit cuts and wheat crackers.

CHICKEN SALAD

1 large hen or
  4 whole breasts
1 cup diced celery
1/2 cup diced sweet
  pickle

1 cup finely chopped
  pecans
1-1½ cups mayonnaise
Pepper, celery salt, and
  onion salt to taste

Boil hen or breasts in salted water until meat
begins to fall off bones. Cool. Remove skin and
bones. Cut chicken with scissors into small pieces.
Add celery, sweet pickle, pecans. Mix. Add mayonnaise to desired consistency. For variety add fresh
white grapes, chopped apple or fresh pineapple bits.
Finely chopped toasted almonds may be substituted
for pecans.

WEDDING PUNCH

3 gallons vanilla
  ice cream
Yellow food coloring,
  optional
3 12 oz. cans frozen
  orange juice concen-
  trate thawed
1 12 oz. cans frozen lime-
  ade concentrate, thawed

3 large cans pineapple
  juice
1 large can apricot nectar
3 liters lemon flavored
  soft drink
2 liters ginger ale

Mash ice cream with potato masher or mix with an
electric mixer in large bowl. Add food coloring if
desired. Mix fruit juices together. Add juice mixture
to softened ice cream. Add lemon flavored soft drink.
Just before serving, add ginger ale. Float ice ring
on top. Yield: 50 4 oz. servings.

To make ice ring: Mash 1/2 gallon vanilla ice cream
with potato masher or mix with electric mixer. Add 2
liters lemon flavored soft drink and yellow food
coloring if desired. Pour into ring mold and freeze.

133

FRENCH PICNIC IN COURTYARD

Marinated Roast Filet of Beef in Brioche

Chive Potato Salad

Assorted Fruits and Cheeses

French Rum Cake

Sangria

MARINATED ROAST FILET OF BEEF

1 filet of beef, 5 to
  6 lb., trimmed
4 to 5 garlic cloves
1 tsp. salt
1 tsp. freshly ground
  black pepper
1/2 tsp hot sauce

1 cup soy sauce
1/2 cup olive oil
1 cup port wine
1 tsp. thyme
1 bay leaf
Bacon strips

Make small gashes in the roast and fill with garlic
cloves, cut in thin slivers. Rub well with salt,
pepper and hot sauce. Marinate overnight in the soy
sauce, olive oil, port wine and herbs, turning several
times. Place on a rack in a shallow roasting pan, top
with a few strips of bacon and roast for 45 minutes
in a 425 degree oven. Baste with the marinade several
times. A meat thermometer inserted into the heaviest
part of the roast should register 125 degrees for rare
and 140-150 degrees for medium. Cool and slice paper
thin for sandwiches.

134

BRIOCHE

2 pkgs. or cakes yeast	1½ tsp salt
1/2 cup lukewarm water	7 eggs
4 cups flour	10 oz. creamed butter
1 tbsp. sugar	

Dissolve yeast in warm water and add 1 cup flour.
Turn out, knead into ball, slash top criss-cross
with knife and drop into lukewarm water. Leave
until dough rises to top. (Less than a minute).
Blend the rest of the flour with sugar and salt
and beat in the whole eggs. Continue stirring
until mixture is smooth, add drained yeast sponge.
Mix in well. Cover with plastic wrap and a cloth.
Set in warm spot to rise until double in bulk.
Punch down dough. Refrigerate dough until you are
ready to bake. (More a necessity than you might
imagine-all that butter gets too warm and when you
punch down the risen dough, you have a pool!)
When you are ready to use the dough, turn it out
onto a floured board and shape into loaf or for
individual brioches, use small fluted molds or
large muffin pans. Shape the dough into balls just
large enough to half fill the molds. Cut a cross
in each ball and insert a small ball of dough to
make the head or crown of the brioche. Cover the
brioches and let them rise in a warm place for
about 30 minutes. Brush them with egg white and
water. Bake for about 15 minutes in a 425 degree
oven.

FRENCH RUM CAKE

1/4 tsp. salt
1 cup sugar
1 tsp rum flavoring
2 eggs, beaten until
  thick and light
1/2 cup milk
1 tbsp. butter
1 cup sifted flour mixed
  with 1 tsp. baking powder

1 cup sugar
1 cup strong coffee
1/8 cup rum
Rum cream filling
Whipped cream
Drained apricot preserves

Add salt, sugar and flavoring to eggs, beat in.
Heat milk and butter in saucepan to boiling. Beat
into egg mixture. Sift flour and baking powder.
Beat into egg mixture. Turn into greased and
floured 9 inch layer cake pan. Bake for 35-40
minutes at 350 degrees. Prepare Coffee Rum Syrup
by dissolving sugar in coffee in saucepan. Bring
to boil and boil for 3 minutes. Cool and add rum.
Spoon syrup slowly over entire surface of warm
cake until syrup is absorbed. Let stand until
cold. Slit cake carefully into 2 layers. Fill
with Rum Cream Filling. Garnish top with whipped
cream and apricot preserves.

RUM CREAM FILLING

1/2 cup sugar
1/4 cup flour
1/8 tsp. salt

2 beaten egg yolks or
  1 beaten egg
2 tbsp. rum

Combine sugar, flour and salt in top of double
boiler. Add milk. Stir over low heat until thick.
Cook over hot water, covered for 10 minutes. Add
small amount of hot mixture to egg yolks. Combine
with remaining hot mixture. Cook for 2 minutes,
stirring constantly. Chill and add rum.
Yield: 8 servings.

CHIVE POTATO SALAD

2 lb, new potatoes,   1 tsp. salt
  cooked, peeled and   1/2 tsp. pepper
  sliced   2 tsp. dijon mustard
1/2 cup mayonnaise   1/4 cup chopped chives

Cook, peel and slice or chop potatoes. Mix
remaining ingredients and toss with potatoes.
Yield: 4 servings.

SANGRIA

See Index for page number of recipe.

NOTES

REMEMBER – Each recipe serves 6 – 8 people unless
              otherwise stated.

GOVERNOR'S WIVES LUNCHEON

> Crab Salad in Avocado Half
>
> Russian Salad Dressing
>
> Molded Grapefruit Pineapple Salad – Hot Rolls
>
> Almond Sheet Dessert
>
> Iced Tea or Coffee

CRAB SALAD IN AVOCADO HALF

2 large avocados, cut
  lengthwise
1 5 oz. can crab meat
1/2 cup mayonnaise

1 cup minced celery
Bottled French dressing
Russian dressing

Peel avocados, marinate in French dressing. Drain.
Fill avocados with crab meat which has been com-
bined with mayonnaise and celery. Serve with
Russian salad dressing.

RUSSIAN SALAD DRESSING

2 cups mayonnaise
1/2 cup minced onion
1/3 cup minced green
  pepper
1 cup finely chopped
  celery

1/2 cup sliced green olives
1 tbsp. Worcestershire
  sauce
1/2 cup chili sauce

Combine all ingredients and keep refrigerated.

MOLDED GRAPEFRUIT PINEAPPLE SALAD

1 3 oz. pkg. lemon
  gelatin
1 cup hot water
1 can crushed pineapple,
  drained

Juice from pineapple
Sections from a grape-
  fruit
1/2 cup diced celery
1/2 cup sliced almonds

Dissolve gelatin in hot water. Add enough cold
water to juice to make 1 cup. Combine gelatin and
juice mixture. When almost congealed, add crushed
pineapple, grapefruit sections, celery and almonds.
Congeal in molds.

ALMOND SHEET DESSERT

1 box confectioners
  sugar
1 cup butter
2 tbsp. almond extract

1 small pkg. shaved
  almonds, toasted
2 cups graham cracker
  crumbs

Cream butter and sugar, add extract, 1 cup cracker
crumbs and toasted almonds. Mix well. Roll out on
cookie sheet in a thin layer (not over 1/2 inch
thick). Refrigerate until ready to use. When ready
to serve, cut in 2 inch squares and top with a
scoop of vanilla ice cream and sprinkle with remaining crumbs. Yield: 18-24 servings.
A pretty party dessert.

Eggs Fermicelli

Sausage Balls in Apple Butter

Hot Fruit Compote   Garlic Cheese Grits

Sour Cream Coffee Cake   Buttermilk Banana Bread

Coffee or Hot Spiced Tea

EGGS FERMICELLI

9 eggs, boiled
1 lb. bacon, sauteed
2 cups grated cheese

3 cups white sauce
Bread crumbs

Grate eggs and crumble bacon. Alternate layers of white sauce, eggs, bacon and cheese to fill a 2 quart casserole. Add extra white sauce and bread crumbs to the top. Bake for 30 minutes in a 350 degree oven. See recipe below for white sauce.

WHITE SAUCE

2 tbsp. butter
1 tbsp. flour
1 tsp. salt
1 tsp. black pepper

1 tsp. Worcestershire sauce
1-1½ cups light cream or milk

In saucepan melt butter. Stir in flour, salt, pepper and Worcestershire sauce. Gradually add light cream or milk and cook over medium heat until creamy or of consistency desired. Yield: 1 cup of sauce.

SAUSAGE BALLS IN APPLE BUTTER

1 large jar apple butter   1 lb. mild sausage

Make marble size sausage balls. Saute in skillet
until cooked. Drain on paper towel. When ready to
serve, heat apple butter in saucepan or chafing dish
and add sausage balls. Keep warm while serving.
Yield: 5 dozen.

GARLIC CHEESE GRITS

1¼ cups grits, uncooked   2 eggs
3½ cups boiling water   1 cup milk
1 roll garlic cheese   1/2 cup cheddar cheese,
1/2 cup butter   grated

Cook grits in boiling water about 30 minutes or
until done. Crumble cheese and butter into cooked
grits. Blend eggs and milk together. Mix egg-milk
mixture with grits. Pour into 2 quart casserole
(greased) and bake for 45 minutes uncovered in a
350 degree oven. Sprinkle with grated cheese
(cheddar) and bake 15 minutes more until cheese is
melted.

BUTTERMILK BANANA BREAD

See Index for page number of recipe.

HOT FRUIT COMPOTE

1 16 oz. can pear halves
1 16 oz. can sliced
  peaches
1 16 oz. can pineapple
  chunks
1 16 oz. can apricot
  halves

12 maraschino cherries
3/4 cup light brown
  sugar
3 tsp. curry powder
1/3 cup melted butter
2/3 cup slivered almonds

Drain all fruit. Add sugar and curry powder to
melted butter. Arrange fruit and nuts in layers
in casserole. Pour butter mixture over all and
bake for 1 hour in a 325 degree oven. Refrigerate
overnight. Reheat at 350 degrees before serving.
Be sure to prepare this a day ahead of serving.
time. Yield: 10-12 servings.

SOUR CREAM COFFEE CAKE

1 cup sour cream
3/4 tsp. soda
1/2 cup brown sugar
1/2 cup chopped pecans
1 tsp. cinnamon
1 cup butter

1 cup sugar
2 eggs
1½ cups all purpose
  flour
1½ tsp. baking powder
1 tsp. vanilla

Mix sour cream and soda and let stand 1 hour. Mix
brown sugar, pecans and cinnamon for topping.
Cream butter and sugar. Add eggs and vanilla and
beat. Add sour cream mixture. Stir in sifted flour
and baking powder. Beat until smooth. Grease and
flour tube cake pan. Alternate layers of batter
and topping. Start with batter and end with topping.
Bake for 40 minutes in a 350 degree oven. Cool in
pan 15 minutes, then remove.

INDEX

BEVERAGES (continued)

BREADS

DESSERTS, CAKES

Almond Sheet Dessert, 139
Angel Cake - Chocolate Sauce, 83
Apricot Nectar Cake, 35
Banana Pineapple Cake, 90
Cheesecake Squares, 110
Chess Cake, 30
Chocolate Cookie Sheet Cake, 82
Dump Cake, 40
Feathery Fudge Cake, 115
Five Flavor Cake, 32
French Rum Cake, 136
Fresh Apple Cake, 81
Fresh Carrot Cake with Cream Cheese Frosting,26
Fudge Cake, 85
Heath Bar Cake, 10
Italian Cream Cake, 111
Kentucky Butter Cake, 81
Lemon Supreme Cake, 24
Orange Pound Cake, 85
Peanut Butter Cake, 116
Pistachio Nut Cake, 114
Poppy Seed Cake, 16
Pound Cake, 84
Pumpkin Squares with Cream Cheese Frosting, 41
Rum Cake, 84
Skillet Coffee Cake, 83
Sour Cream Coffee Cake, 142
Sour Cream Pound Cake, 19
Springtime Torte, 90
Strawberry Angel Food Cake, 86
Tangy Citrus Cake, 28

DESSERTS, PIES

Bourbon and Chocolate Pecan Pie, 112
Buttermilk Pie, 8
Buttermilk Raisin Pie, 88

DESSERTS, PIES (continued)

DESSERTS, SWEETS

ENTREES

Baked Chicken Piquant with Rice, 127
Baked Fish with Shrimp - Parmesan Sauce, 107
Beef Burgundy, 64
Brunswick Stew, 70
Buffet Meat Loaf, 104
Buffet Stroganoff, 103
Carolyn's Chicken, 107
Cheese Souffle, 39
Chicken Breasts in Wine, 64
Chicken Casserole, 103
Corn and Ham Chowder, 20
Creamed Chicken, 13
Creole Pork Chops, 66
Easy Jambalaya, 104
Eggs Fermicelli, 140
French Pot Roast, 66
Fried Chicken, 119
Ham Casserole, 65
Ham Loaf, 102
Hot Baked Chicken Salad, 65
Hot Tuna Sandwich with Mushroom Cheese
    Sauce, 33
Marinated Roast Fillet of Beef, 134
Melange of Chipped Beef and Mushrooms
    over Chinese Noodles, 31
Mexican Casserole, 21
Miss Daisy's Beef Casserole, 25
Parmesan Round Steak, 68
Quiche Lorraine, 35
Sausage Casserole, 68
Seafood Casserole, 132
Seafood and Rice Casserole, 69
Shrimp Creole, 9
Split Pea Soup with Sherry, 41
Steak Oriental, 67
Sweet and Sour Chicken, 102
Sweet and Sour Meatballs, 105
Tearoom Chili, 19

ENTREES (continued)

Tuna Cashew Casserole, 67
Turkey Divan, 7
Turkey Tetrazzini, 105
Veal Parmesan, 69
Welsh Rabbit, 29
Wild Rice and Oyster Casserole, 106

SALADS

Apricot Salad, 55
Bing Cherry Salad, 55
Black-Eyed Pea Salad – Greek Style, 56
Carter s Court Salad Bowl, 11
Chicken Salad, 133
Chive Potato Salad, 137
Christmas Ribbon Salad, 94
Congealed Beet Salad, 31
Congealed Cucumber Salad, 9
Congealed Green Pea Salad, 56
Congealed Spiced Peach Salad, 93
Corn Relish, 34
Crab Salad in Avocado Half, 138
Festive Cranberry Salad, 14
Festive Shrimp Salad with Sour Cream
  Dressing, 27
Fresh Fruit Bowl, 23
Frozen Cherry Salad, 7
Garden Tomato Stuffed with Tearoom Tuna
  Salad, 17
Grandmother Hubbard's Frozen Fruit Salad, 37
Ham Salad, 120
Honey – French Dressing, 11
Hot Fruit Compote, 142
Lime Fluff, 94
Marinated Carrots, 14
Marinated Vegetables, 95
Molded Grapefruit Pineapple Salad, 139
Orange Sherbert Salad, 57
Party Salad Topping, 58

SALADS (continued)

Peppermint Stick Candy Salad, 57
Pineapple Salad Supreme, 56
Pink Artic Freeze, 39
Poppy Seed Dressing, 23
Sauerkraut Salad, 95
Seven Cup Salad, 57
Shrimp Aspic Mold with Horseradish
  Dressing, 15
Shrimp Mold, 126
Strawberry - Lemon Congealed Salad, 93
Summer Salad, 58
Tomato Aspic, 28
Tuna Mousse, 96
Waldorf Salad, 29

VEGETABLES

Asparagus and English Pea Casserole, 97
Baked Limas with Sour Cream, 60
Best Baked Beans, 59
Broccoli with Horseradish Dressing, 60
Broccoli Rice Casserole, 97
Carrot Raisin Casserole, 101
Corn Pudding, 100
Easy Spinach Casserole, 99
Eggplant Casserole, 100
Eggplant Souffle, 61
Garlic Cheese Grits, 141
Green Bean Casserole, 59
Green Beans and Water Chestnuts, 127
Herbed Tomatoes, 63
Onion Casserole, 61
Oriental Vegetable Casserole, 99
Party Squash, 61
Quick and Easy Peas, 101
Rice Supreme, 98
Spinach and Artichoke Casserole, 62

VEGETABLES (Continued)

GIFT ORDER BLANK

Daisy's Uptown
126 Church Street Mall
Nashville, Tennessee 37219

Please send me _____ copies of RECIPES FROM MISS
DAISY'S at $6.95 per copy, plus $1.75 postage and
handling for each shipment (even if more than one book
is mailed), to friends whose names and addresses are
listed below. (Tennessee residents, please add $.54
per copy sales tax.) Make checks payable to Daisy's
Uptown and mail to the above address. With each book,
Daisy will include a gift card signed with your name.

Your name _____

Street Address _____

City, State, and Zip _____

Send cookbooks to:
— —

Name _____

Street Address _____

City, State, and Zip _____

Name _____

Street Address _____

City, State, and Zip _____

Name _____

Street Addresss _____

City, State, and Zip _____

GIFT ORDER BLANK

Daisy's Uptown
126 Church Street Mall
Nashville, Tennessee 37219

Please send me _____ copies of RECIPES FROM MISS
DAISY'S at $6.95 per copy, plus $1.75 postage and
handling for each shipment (even if more than one book
is mailed), to friends whose names and addresses are
listed below. (Tennessee residents, please add $.54
per copy sales tax.) Make checks payable to Daisy's
Uptown and mail to the above address. With each book,
Daisy will include a gift card signed with your name.

Your name _____

Street Address _____

City, State, and Zip _____

Send cookbooks to:
_ _

Name _____

Street Address _____

City, State, and Zip _____

Name _____

Street Address _____

City, State, and Zip _____

Name _____

Street Addresss _____

City, State, and Zip _____

GIFT ORDER BLANK

Daisy's Uptown
126 Church Street Mall
Nashville, Tennessee 37219

Please send me _____ copies of RECIPES FROM MISS
DAISY'S at $6.95 per copy, plus $1.75 postage and
handling for each shipment (even if more than one book
is mailed), to friends whose names and addresses are
listed below. (Tennessee residents, please add $.54
per copy sales tax.) Make checks payable to Daisy's
Uptown and mail to the above address. With each book,
Daisy will include a gift card signed with your name.

Your name _____

Street Address _____

City, State, and Zip _____

Send cookbooks to:
— —

Name _____

Street Address _____

City, State, and Zip _____

Name _____

Street Address _____

City, State, and Zip _____

Name _____

Street Addresss _____

City, State, and Zip _____

GIFT ORDER BLANK

Daisy's Uptown
126 Church Street Mall
Nashville, Tennessee 37219

Please send me _____ copies of RECIPES FROM MISS
DAISY'S at $6.95 per copy, plus $1.75 postage and
handling for each shipment (even if more than one book
is mailed), to friends whose names and addresses are
listed below. (Tennessee residents, please add $.54
per copy sales tax.) Make checks payable to Daisy's
Uptown and mail to the above address. With each book,
Daisy will include a gift card signed with your name.

Your name _____

Street Address _____

City, State, and Zip _____

Send cookbooks to:
_ _

Name _____

Street Address _____

City, State, and Zip _____

Name _____

Street Address _____

City, State, and Zip _____

Name _____

Street Addresss _____

City, State, and Zip _____